Home Decluttering Done Best for Success!

Your Complete 90 Day Step-By-Step Guide to Creating a Calm, Well-Organized and Stress-Free Home.

Charity H Jones

3eye publishing

Home Decluttering Done Best for Success!

Charity H Jones

© Copyright 2023 – All rights reserved.

The contents of this book may not be reproduced, duplicated, or transmitted without direct written permission from the author

Under no circumstances will any legal responsibility or blame be held against the publisher for any reparation, damages, or monetary loss due to the information herein, either directly or indirectly.

Legal Notice:

this book is copyright protected. This is only for personal use. You cannot amend, distribute, sell, use, quote, or paraphrase any part or the content within this book without the consent of the author.

Disclaimer Notice:

Please note the information contained within this document is for educational and entertainment purposes only. Every attempt has been made to provide accurate, up-to-date, and reliable complete information. No warranties of any kind are expressed or implied. Readers acknowledge that the author is not engaging in the rendering of legal, financial, medical or professional advice. The content of this book has been derived from various sources. Please consult a licensed professional before attempting any techniques outlined in this book.

By reading this document, the reader agrees that under no circumstances is the author responsible for any losses, direct or indirect, which are incurred as a result of the use of the information contained within this document, including, but not limited to, -errors, omissions, or inaccuracies.

Book Cover by Olina@olinart

1st edition 2023

Contents

Welcome to Home Decluttering Done Best for Success! — IV
1. Understanding the Clutter-Stress Connection — 1
2. The Art of Mindful Decluttering — 12
3. Emotional Attachment and Letting Go — 20
4. Creating a Declutterng Plan — 32
5. The 90-Day Home Decluttering Program — 43
6. Living Room — 52
7. Dining Room — 58
8. Kitchen — 67
9. Bathroom — 73
10. Bedroom — 81
11. Attics, Basements, and Store Rooms — 88
12. Sustainable Decluttering and Responsible Disposal — 96
13. Program Conclusion — 104
14. Bonus Chapter: Nurturing a Mindful Home — 109

Acknowledgements — 117
About the Author — 118

Welcome to Home Decluttering Done Best for Success!

Welcome my fellow declutters.

Thank you! It's a genuine pleasure to have you right here, right now, taking that precious time out from your busy, hectic lives to hold my book in your hands or at least to scroll through it digitally :) You have made a great choice. But of course, I would say that you say, but really... you have.

We have all grown accustomed to being busy, rushing around like headless chickens, getting on with our lives, and accumulating more and more things as we go. Without thinking or wishing it we amass stuff, lots and lots of stuff around us. Possession overload! Over time these possessions start to weigh us down, dragging at our ankles, and sapping our strength. Trust me when I say, I've been there, and it was enough to drive me completely bonkers. How the hell did I, or we, end up with so much stuff?

It got to a point where I would dread coming home each evening. To open the front door only to be met by the mass of mess and clutter that lay in wait just inside the threshold. Shoes. Coats. Bags. Stuff! A chaotic sea of clutter that would somehow magically regenerate itself every day which no one else seemed to notice! I loathed the wardrobe, the looming beast of chaos that used to fill me with a sense of dread every time I approached it. And I felt the utter frustration of desperately searching for something so simple, like the tv remote, the car keys, the cat! Only to have them buried beneath an avalanche of belongings.

I get it. Boy, do I get it! You see, I've experienced it all. The frustration and overwhelm of possessions crammed into every nook and cranny of my poor, long-suffering home. I've felt the anger and desperation as the clutter became invisible to the rest of my family as if its very familiarity meant that it was just a part of our daily lives. Something to just step over or mindlessly move aside.Something simply to get used to. Oh, how I longed for them to see what I saw, to understand the chaos that was slowly engulfing us. To feel what I was feeling.

I won't sugarcoat it; there were moments when I felt utterly defeated. The weight of the clutter was suffocating, making me question my sanity and my self-worth. At my lowest I found myself in the darkest corners of despair, contemplating things that were stupid and unthinkable. I was truly and utterly miserable, but just like the clutter it seemed that no one had time to notice. I knew deep inside that I had to make a change but somehow that change was always being delayed. There was always a reason why next week or the week following would have to do. I was simply too busy to deal with it right now. Postponed by procrastination. Deferred by the overwhelming dread of tackling such an insidious beast. My family was growing and so too were the possessions that we had somehow convinced ourselves that we needed. But our house was a fixed size. The walls did not expand in the same way as the clutter did. The car moved out. Yes, it was literally evicted from the garage. I know that many people's garages are the first to be sacrificed in a bid to combat clutter, but the spare bedroom quickly followed. Nothing was sacred and nothing seemed enough. Our actual physical living space began to shrink around us as more piles of things arrived and built up. I started to feel deeply ashamed of the state that our home had become. I felt that it was my fault. Surely I should be able to keep house. It wasn't even that big! I began shunning having friends over for fear that they would think badly of me. Afraid that their opinions would make me feel even lower than I was already feeling. My relationship started to suffer. We would argue about silly things that seemed suddenly intensified and inflated as we ran out of room to make space for our lives. Then one day I stood there looking at the untidy piles of crap everywhere with tears filling my eyes and I had to decide. Was I going to surrender and call it a day? It would mean leaving it all behind and simply walking away to protect my sanity. Or was I going to do something about it? Surely I was in one of the best places to fight back. I bloody designed clean and clear living spaces for a living! I wiped the tears from my eyes, gritted my teeth and there and then chose to do something about it. Everything else was too important and precious for me to lose. I got angry not just with myself but with the very things that were making me feel so bad. I took action. Decisive action. I focused on the area in front of me and started clearing, cleaning, tidying, and organizing. At the same time, I began planning and deciding how I would ensure that it would never revert to being the life-sucking quagmire of clutter it had become. I vowed never to let clutter claim me as its victim. I knew that I really had no other choice but to make it my mission to find a way out, to break free from the suffocating prison that my home had sadly become over the years. For my own sake and that of my family! I began decluttering.

And now, here I am, standing before you, reaching out my hand to help you to escape that same prison. This book, my friends, is my lifeline to you. It's filled with the lessons I've learned, the strategies I've developed, and the secrets I've uncovered on my journey to decluttering and liberation. Together I promise you we can conquer the clutter, banish the chaos, and create a sanctuary of calm and serenity within your home. Believe me, it really can be done. It's not always easy it can be bloody hard, but I will attempt in this book to give it to you real and help you get to where you want to be. To reach a place where clutter does not impact your home, your life, and your well-being and where suddenly organization and calm aid your family's success in life. And I promise you it will. By taking up this book and reading its contents you have already moved forward. It's your first step and I will help you take many more as we walk hand in hand on this journey together.

In the following chapters, we'll delve deep into the heart of the clutter conundrum. We'll explore practical tips, mindset shifts, and actionable steps that will revolutionize the way you approach decluttering. We'll address the pain points that have burdened you for far too long, from overwhelmed spaces to emotional attachments, and provide you with the tools you need to overcome them.

But hopefully, you will find that this book is more than just a guide. It's a companion, a friend who understands your struggles and walks alongside you. Together, we'll navigate the messy terrain, celebrate victories small and large, and conquer any obstacle that dares cross our path. By the time we reach the final page, you'll not only have a clutter-free home but a renewed sense of peace, a sanctuary that reflects your true self. Oh, and we will do this together in just 90 days!

So, my dear friend, are you ready to embark on this transformative journey? Are you ready to bid farewell to the chaos of clutter and reclaim your space, your sanity, and your life? Trust me when I say, there's a brighter, clutter-free future waiting just around the corner. Let's dive in, hand in hand, and discover the liberation that awaits us.

Chapter One

Understanding the Clutter-Stress Connection

"Clutter is not just physical stuff. It's old ideas, toxic relationships, and bad habits. Clutter is anything that does not support your better self." - **Eleanor Brownn**[1]

Introduction to The Clutter-Stress Connection

Hey there, fellow clutter warriors! Welcome to Day 1, Chapter 1 of our incredible journey together toward an organized and stress-free home. Brace yourself as we embark on a transformational adventure that will unravel the enigmatic bond between clutter and our mental well-being. Prepare to be captivated as we delve deep into the untamed realms

---

1. Brownn, E. (2016). The Unseen Art of Decluttering: The Ultimate Guide to Clearing Out, Organizing, and Revitalizing Your Home. CreateSpace Independent Publishing Platform.

of chaos and discover the profound impact it has on our daily lives. Together, we'll unlock the keys to a calm and harmonious existence, where our homes become havens of tranquility and our souls find solace.

Amidst the hustle and bustle of our busy lives, it's easy to overlook the clutter that creeps in silently, infiltrating our surroundings and tugging at our sanity. But fret not, my friends, for you are not alone in this battle. Clutter has a way of weaving itself into the fabric of our lives, leaving us feeling overwhelmed and yearning for a respite from the chaos. I've been there, one minute we had moved into our beautiful new home with our somewhat chaotic and always super busy family, and the next minute life and all that comes with it took over. Once our possessions from our past lives had neatly filled the inner spaces and we had decorated the way we wanted, we quickly started to add. A little here, a little there. Maybe that sofa was a little too large for that room but we bought it anyway and added a chair. We squeezed in a dining table that was big enough to seat ten. Ten! There were only four of us! When we first moved in we didn't even know six friends! The cupboards quickly become over full and piles of possessions would start to pop up in the most unlikely of places. Things we bought would be added to the things we brought. Things didn't get thrown out whilst other things got added frequently. Sooner than you would ever think our shiny new home was no longer the happy place we had envisaged but instead became a suffocating mire, a sea of possessions beneath which I was starting to mentally drown. If you are feeling the same or hopefully you are not yet in that state of affairs but may see it looming ahead, well then it's my fervent desire to guide you toward the light of serenity and inner calm that can be had with some effort, determination but most of all a bloody big dollop of understanding.

In this chapter, we'll journey together through the depths of clutter-induced stress, unraveling its grip on our minds and hearts. We'll illuminate the dark recesses clutter thrives in, shedding light on the hidden toll it takes on our mental well-being.

Why are we starting with this you may ask? Well, I have found that to move forward we first need to understand where we are and how we got here and above all recognize how it is affecting us, mind, body, and soul. Once we fully understand the tenacious grip that clutter has upon us we can fight back. And we can and will win! So it's time to lift the veil and confront the clutter-stress connection head-on.

Prepare to be enthralled as we uncover the hidden ways clutter chips away at our peace, leaving us feeling drained and weighed down by the weight of everything we own. From the scattered surfaces that breed anxiety to the cluttered closets that trigger a sense of deep unease, we'll explore the profound impact clutter has on our daily lives. It's time to take back control and reclaim the serenity that is rightfully ours.

But fear not, for as we dive into the depths of clutter-induced stress, we'll also unveil the transformative power that decluttering has. We'll unlock the door to a calm living environment where our minds can thrive, our spirits can soar, and our souls can find solace. Decluttering is not just about creating physical space; it's a gateway to cultivating inner calm and finding harmony in our lives.

Throughout this chapter, we'll navigate the intricate landscape of clutter-induced stress, recognizing its signs and understanding its impact. We'll uncover the remarkable benefits that await us when we summon the courage to embark on the decluttering journey. Together, we'll forge a path toward a calm and organized living environment, where clarity reigns supreme and stress becomes a distant memory.

So, my fellow clutter warriors, are you ready to seize control of your surroundings, restore balance to your lives, and embark on a transformational journey toward inner peace? Let us embark on this extraordinary adventure together, where the clutter-stress connection will be unraveled, and the path to a calmer, more fulfilling life will be illuminated.

Onward we go toward a clutter-free existence filled with joy, serenity, and a renewed zest for life!

Clutter's Impact on Our Mental Well-being

Let's now journey deep into the labyrinth of clutter and unravel the intricate web it weaves within our minds and souls. Prepare to confront the profound impact it has on our mental well-being, for the battle begins on the battleground we call home. Within the walls that should offer solace and serenity, chaos takes hold, casting its suffocating shadow over our lives. But fret not, for within the darkness lies the key to our liberation.

In our modern world, where possessions accumulate like waves crashing upon the shore, it's all too easy to underestimate the toll that clutter exacts upon our mental state. We may dismiss the piles of possessions as mere inconveniences, oblivious to the invisible weight they place upon our shoulders. But hidden within the cluttered corners of our homes lie stressors that chip away at our well-being, subtly eroding the tranquility we crave. Before we jump into clearing and cleaning, organizing and decluttering we must make time to identify a few things first. We need to gain understanding and use it to our advantage for the battles to come. Let's explore together.

Waking up in a bedroom engulfed in disorder is no way to start your day, right? Seeing clothes hanging haphazardly from every surface and forgotten items littering the floor like scattered memories will drive you to distraction. The mere sight of clutter assaults our senses, sending signals of unease to our weary minds even if we expel a lot of energy just trying to block them all out.

How do you feel when you wake up?

What are you met with the minute you open your eyes?

What lurks in the early morning light to interrupt your calm?

Can you remember a time when your home environment was clear and peaceful? Where everything was in its place? If you can then you know it did exist and the feelings you felt at the time. If not then trust me, it can and the difference will be remarkable. Our surroundings mirror the disarray within, intensifying the whirlwind of thoughts and emotions that swirl inside us. Indeed looking back I think that clutter acted as a sort of catalyst and outward expression for the disarray my whole life was plummeting towards. It felt scary. It felt out of control.

So it is not just the visual assault that takes its toll on us. The impact of clutter reaches far deeper, penetrating the realms of our subconscious and influencing our daily lives. Each item vies for attention, competing for a place in our already over-taxed minds. The constant barrage of stimuli overwhelms our cognitive capacity, leaving us drained and unable to focus on what truly matters.

As the clutter accumulates, so too does the weight upon our shoulders. The burden of unfinished tasks, unresolved decisions, and misplaced belongings hangs heavy in the air, breeding a sense of helplessness and lack of control. We find ourselves trapped in a vicious cycle, where the more we accumulate, the more our mental well-being suffers.

Amid this chaos, it becomes increasingly challenging to find respite and nurture our inner peace. Our homes, once sanctuaries of solace, become battlegrounds where stress and anxiety wage war on our serenity. The disarray that surrounds us seeps into our very souls, fueling a constant state of unease and restlessness. For me, it felt like drowning beneath rough waves in a heavy sea. Each pile of possessions adding to the size of the swell. With each day feeling harder than the last.

But dear reader, take heart, for this battle is not one fought in vain. By digging into the depths of clutter's impact on our mental well-being, we unveil the power to reclaim our homes and restore our harmony. By understanding the intricate dance between clutter and our minds, we can arm ourselves with the knowledge to overcome its grip.

In the chapters that follow, we will embark on a transformative journey by shedding light on the hidden corners of clutter-induced stress and unveiling the path to inner calm. We will explore the signs that clutter-induced stress manifests within us, enabling us to recognize its presence and take decisive action. And as we delve deeper, we will discover the multitude of benefits that await us on the other side of decluttering—a calm and serene living environment that nurtures our mental as well as physical well-being.

So, brace yourself, for the battle against clutter-induced stress has just begun. Together, we shall confront the chaos that threatens our peace, armed with knowledge, determination and the unwavering belief that an organized and stress-free home is within our grasp. Let us embark on this journey, for within its winding path lies the promise of inner calm and a life free from the clutches of clutter.

Recognizing the Signs of Clutter-Induced Stress

Amidst the clamor of our daily lives, clutter whispers its insidious secrets, leaving subtle imprints on our well-being. Let us now tune our ears to the quiet language it speaks, revealing the signs of clutter-induced stress that often go unnoticed. As we embark on this journey of self-discovery, let's take a moment to reflect upon our surroundings.

Do you hear the echoes of clutter-induced stress in the rooms you inhabit?

This **5-minute exercise** should be done in conjunction with the training in part 3.

Find a comfy chair in a quiet space away from noise and interference. Try to relax. Take your shoes off and ensure that your feet are flat on the floor. Ensure that your body is equally and well supported. Are you sitting comfortably? Good. Take a deep breath…

Calm yourself and regulate your heartbeat.

Keep breathing, deeply drawing in fresh air through your nose

Holding it for 5 seconds …………

Now exhale gradually through your mouth.

Breathe in deeply

Hold for 5 seconds……………

Breathe out

Keep doing this and at the same time try to clear your mind of inner distractions. Relax into the chair and feel your body's weight gently supported. Keep breathing deeply. Feel the air filling your lungs and your entire being from the ends of your fingers to the tips of your toes. Feel the stressors begin to fall away. Keep doing this for a couple of minutes until you start to feel really relaxed and comfortable and fully in the moment.

Now keep your mind closed to distractions, envision your home, look beyond its superficial appearance, and venture into the depths of your living space. Can you recall the exact moment when clutter first tiptoed into your life? Was it a slow and gradual accumulation? A stealthy arrival that at first, you didn't notice but once it had gained a foothold you suddenly became aware of its toxic existence. Or did it arrive all at once, in a whirlwind of chaos? If so, what was that single event?

Keep it pictured in your mind.

Now, recall the impact that clutter had on you, not just visually or physically, but emotionally and mentally as well. How did it make you feel?

Was it just an initial inconvenience or did it quickly start to weigh heavily on your spirit, draining your energy?

When did the clutter start to increase? As it did, did it start to make you feel differently? Did you start to feel overwhelmed? Did you find yourself caught in a constant battle against it, striving to create order amidst the ever-growing chaos? What feelings surface as you explore this in your mind?

Think back to the moments when clutter first disrupted the harmony within your home. Did it affect your interactions with others? With family, friends, partners, and loved ones? Did it hinder the ease of communication and connection, creating barriers within your family dynamics? Reflect on the times when clutter became a source of tension, a silent instigator of discord and frustration. Is it having that very same effect today?

Did you notice how clutter spilled over into other areas of your life, infiltrating your thoughts and emotions even when you were away from home? Consider the mental burden it imposed, and how it occupied precious space in your mind, leaving little room for clarity and focus. Do you find yourself grappling with a constant sense of unease, an underlying restlessness that lingers throughout your day? Is that how you feel today?

And what of the impact on those who share your living space? How did the gathering clutter affect them? Did they simply ignore it? Did they rile against it or did it dampen their spirits, making it difficult for them to find solace and peace within the home? Reflect on the relationships that were strained by the weight of clutter, the missed opportunities for connection and joy that clutter obscured. Do you recognize any of these thoughts?

Do you feel sadness? Do you feel anger?

Close your eyes and consider all of this for a few minutes. Gather up those feelings.

Now, open your eyes and bring your attention back to the present moment.

Are there echoes of recognition within your own experiences? Can you see the signs of clutter-induced stress that have quietly nestled themselves within the fabric of your life? Take a deep breath and know that you are truly not alone. These feelings we will do our darndest to remove from our lives as we work together. These negativities we will eradicate! We will not permit them to exist, sapping our mental fortitude and ruining our lives. When we finish this program these feelings will be finished too!

Recognizing the signs of clutter-induced stress is the first step toward reclaiming your serenity. By acknowledging the impact clutter has on your well-being and the well-being of those around you, you gain the power to create change. Together, we will explore and establish strategies to overcome clutter-induced stress and forge a path toward a calmer and more harmonious existence.

The Benefits of Decluttering

Amidst the wreckage of clutter, a glimmer of hope emerges, beckoning us toward a far brighter future. As we embark on the journey of decluttering, we unleash a powerful transformation that extends far beyond mere tidiness. Brace yourself, for the rewards that await us on this path, are nothing short of extraordinary.

Let's now repeat the exercise in part 2. This will take **5 minutes.**

Find that comfy chair. Get comfortable once again. Take your shoes off and place your feet flat on the floor. Close your mind to other distractions and breathe in deeply through your nose holding your breath for 5 seconds before expelling it through your mouth. Keep repeating. As you expel the air you are also expelling all negativity and distractions. Feel the chair support you. Feel it embrace you. Feel secure. Keep breathing deeply.

Once you feel more relaxed and in the moment imagine the following scenario: You step through your front door into your home, your sanctuary, and immediately feel a sense of serenity wash over you. The burden of clutter has been lifted. Your house is clear and clean, organized, and clutter-free. You have time to breathe and move around freely with ease. Nothing gets in your way. Everything is in its place and you know where everything is (even the cat if you have one). There's a feeling of calmness that washes over you, freeing you from the stresses and strains of the world outside. This is your oasis of peacefulness. In this calm living environment, your mind finds respite, liberated from the constant barrage of visual chaos that once existed. Your space is now yours and it becomes a canvas upon which you can create and thrive.

Close your eyes and spend a few minutes enjoying that feeling. Explore your home. Travel through its rooms reveling in the calmness and order of things. Seeing all the space that lies between its walls available for you to appreciate. Let it fill you up inside, bringing serenity and peace to every part of your body.

Now, open your eyes and bring your attention back to the present moment. Keep those feelings inside and know that these are the feelings that we will nurture and ensure thrive as we reclaim your home together.

Know with absolute certainty that the benefits of decluttering extend far beyond mere aesthetics. As you release the physical clutter, you release the mental weight that has held you captive for so long. Clearing your space opens up room for clarity and mental well-being to flourish. You'll find that decision-making becomes easier, as the distractions of excess are stripped away. Your mind becomes a sanctuary, a fertile ground for inspiration and creativity to take root.

In this newfound order, you'll discover that productivity becomes your trusted companion. With a clutter-free environment, your focus sharpens, allowing you to tackle tasks with greater efficiency and effectiveness. You'll no longer waste precious time searching for misplaced items or sifting through piles of stuff. Instead, you'll experience a newfound sense of control and accomplishment, paving the way for a life of purpose and fulfillment.

But it is not just you who will benefit from the transformation. Your loved ones, too, will reap the rewards of a far calmer living environment. As clutter retreats, relationships flourish. Your home becomes a space that nurtures connection and fosters harmonious interactions. Family members can breathe more freely, unburdened by the weight of chaos. The energy within your home transforms, becoming a haven of love, laughter, and shared experiences.

Beyond the walls of your home, the ripple effects of decluttering will extend into all aspects of your life. The newfound clarity and peace you have cultivated will undoubtedly spill over into your work, your relationships, and your overall well-being. You'll find yourself approaching challenges with renewed energy, resilience, and grace. Your sense of self-worth blossoms, as you realize the immense power you hold to shape your surroundings and your destiny.

So, my fellow traveler, let us embrace the transformation that awaits us. Let us step into the realm of calm and reclaim our lives from the clutches of clutter. As we declutter our physical spaces, know that we are also decluttering our minds and hearts, creating a fertile ground for joy, creativity, and a renewed sense of purpose. The path may not always be easy, but the rewards that lie ahead are worth every step. Together, let us curate a calm living environment and unlock the true potential that resides within us all.

Chapter Two

The Art of Mindful Decluttering

"Clear your physical space. Clear your mental space. Clear your emotional space. Clarity is the key to manifesting your dreams." - **Marie Kondo**[1]

Introduction to Mindfulness

In our pursuit of an organized and stress-free home, we often find ourselves caught in a cycle of constant busyness, racing against time to tidy up our surroundings. We yearn for a sanctuary, a place of tranquility where our minds can find solace amidst the chaos of our daily lives. It is in this pursuit that we discover the transformative path of mindful decluttering—a profound journey that goes beyond mere physical tidiness.

Mindfulness, rooted in ancient wisdom and practices, offers us a gateway to approach decluttering with intention, presence, and a deeper awareness of our inner landscape. It invites us to cultivate a deeper connection

---

1. Kondo, M. (2016). Spark Joy: An Illustrated Master Class on the Art of Organizing and Tidying Up. Ten Speed Press.

to our belongings, to explore the intricate interplay between our external environment and our internal state of being.

As we embark on this chapter, we open ourselves to the power of mindfulness as part of the art of decluttering. We shift our focus from the mere act of discarding items to the exploration of our relationship with them. Mindful decluttering encourages us to bring a heightened sense of awareness to our possessions, to question the stories that they hold, and to evaluate their impact on our lives.

Approaching Decluttering with Intention and Presence

In the realm of mindfulness decluttering, each item becomes an opportunity for self-reflection. We pause and ask ourselves: Does this object serve a purpose in my life? Does it bring me joy and align with my values? By infusing intention and presence into our decluttering process, we cultivate a deeper connection with our surroundings and gain a profound understanding of what truly matters to us.

As we navigate our homes, we encounter the treasures we've accumulated over the years. Mindfulness invites us to observe our emotional responses to these possessions. We explore the attachments we've formed and the stories that have woven themselves into the fabric of our lives. With gentle curiosity, we peel back the layers and discover the true essence of our relationship with our belongings.

Mindfulness teaches us the art of letting go without judgment or guilt. We learn to release the items that no longer serve us, knowing that their departure creates space for new possibilities and growth. Through this intentional act of decluttering, we invite a sense of lightness and freedom into our lives. We liberate ourselves from the burden of excess, allowing our homes to breathe and our minds to expand. Without truly being able to understand the reason something has been held on to for so long, we can never feel fully confident in our decisions over its future. I found letting go of possessions really difficult as did Paul, my husband. We had kept the things for a reason even if we couldn't always recall what that exact reason was. It was an irrational anxiety to let it go to make space for something new, or just to make space. And it was all the more anxious because I didn't truly understand the items' worth, or lack of it, to me.

So mindfulness decluttering extends beyond physical possessions. It permeates our thoughts, emotions, and daily habits. We cultivate mindfulness in our decision-making, becoming more conscious of the impact our choices have on our environment and our overall well-being. We learn to distinguish between genuine needs and mere desires, aligning our actions with our values and reducing the impulse to accumulate unnecessary belongings. This will serve us well in the future as we strive to maintain our hard-won freedom from clutter.

By embracing mindfulness in our decluttering journey, we embark on a path of self-discovery and transformation. We create space not only in our homes but also in our hearts and minds. As we let go of the excess, we create room for clarity, inspiration, and a deep sense of inner calm.

In the next sections of this chapter, we will explore deeper into the practical techniques and strategies that infuse mindfulness into the decluttering process. We will discover how self-care practices and stress reduction strategies can support us on this transformative journey.

Get ready to embark on a path of mindful decluttering, where each decision is infused with intention, and each moment holds the potential for profound change.

Self-Care Practices and Stress Reduction Strategies

In this section, we explore practical self-care practices and stress reduction strategies that can accompany us on our decluttering adventure. These techniques will help us maintain our well-being, foster a positive mindset, and infuse joy into the process.

One powerful practice is to start each decluttering session with a moment of mindfulness. Try this: Take a few deep breaths, grounding yourself in the present moment. Set an intention for the decluttering session, reminding yourself of the benefits that await you on the other side. Close your eyes and visualize what you will achieve. Take a few moments to feel what completing that decluttering session will bring to you. Feel the joy fill your body and feed upon it to energize your being and provide purpose. By bringing mindfulness into the equation, you can approach decluttering with a sense of calm, clarity, and intent.

As you engage with your belongings, notice the sensations in your body and the thoughts that arise. Pay attention to any feelings of attachment, resistance, or overwhelm. Allow yourself to fully experience these emotions without judgment. Don't back away from them. The difference here is that you are not afraid of feeling a connection or a doubt about clearing the item out. You are open to exploring its emotional value and willing to accept that after such introspection it may hold absolutely none. Remember, decluttering is not just about physical objects; it's an opportunity for self-discovery and personal growth.

To infuse self-care into the process, consider creating a ritual or setting up a cozy decluttering environment. Light a scented candle, play soothing music, or surround yourself with items that bring you comfort and inspiration. Engage your senses and create an atmosphere that supports your well-being. This intentional environment will enhance your focus and create a nurturing space for you to begin the decluttering journey ahead.

Throughout the decluttering process, it's important to listen to your body and honor its needs. Take regular breaks to stretch, hydrate, and nourish yourself with healthy snacks. Physical movement can also be a form of self-care, so consider integrating short bursts of exercise or stretching into your decluttering routine. These moments of self-care not only rejuvenate your body but also refresh your mind, allowing you to approach the task with renewed energy and focus. When I tackled an area of my home I would often do it in short bursts of high activity. Getting stuck into a specific area to clear it as I went without getting too bogged down in the sentimentality of it all. Then I would review what I had achieved. Take a break, walk away, and then return to look and consider what I had removed. Yes, you guessed it… several things were later returned to the 'keep' pile but overall I felt that certainly during the early stages of decluttering, good progress was made.

Another powerful strategy is to practice gratitude as you declutter. Express appreciation for the items that have served you well and those that hold sentimental value. Say a heartfelt goodbye to the items you choose to release, acknowledging the role that they have had in your life and the lessons they have taught you. Cultivating gratitude during the decluttering process shifts your perspective from one of scarcity to one of abundance, fostering a positive and more empowered mindset.

Lastly, remember to celebrate your progress along the way. This is super important! Recognize and acknowledge the efforts you have made, no matter how small they may seem. Treat yourself with kindness and compassion throughout the process. Reward yourself with moments of joy, whether it's enjoying a cup of tea, indulging in a favorite activity, or simply taking a moment to appreciate the newfound space and clarity in your home. I found that focusing on a specific space, say a cupboard or the backend of a room was a good way to break things down into bite-sized chunks and once they were fully decluttered I stood back and congratulated myself. Remember to take the time to get up, dust yourself down, stand back, and focus on your achievement. See how good that particular area now looks. It doesn't matter about anything outside of that because that is the area of your success! You did that. You made a difference!

By incorporating self-care practices and stress reduction strategies into your decluttering journey, you create a harmonious balance between external and internal transformation. You nourish your well-being, enhance your resilience, and infuse the process with a sense of joy and fulfillment. Embrace these practices as valuable companions on your path to mindful decluttering, and let them support you in creating a home and life that truly resonate with your authentic self.

Promoting a holistic approach to decluttering

Now we will explore more practical advice and exercises that promote a holistic approach to decluttering, one that considers the profound connection between both the mind and body. By integrating these practices into your journey, you will embark on a transformative path toward greater clarity, serenity, and well-being.

- **Mindful Sorting**: As you declutter, practice mindful sorting. Hold each item in your hands and observe how it makes you feel. Does it bring you joy, or does it weigh you down? Does it have no emotional impact on you at all? Cultivate a discerning eye and let go of possessions that no longer serve a purpose or align with your values. Trust your intuition and make decisions that support your well-being. This process can be as fast as you want and often gets far quicker the more you practice it.

- **Emotional Release Ritual**: Recognize that letting go of physical clutter often comes with emotional attachments. Create a ritual that allows you to acknowledge and release these emotions. It could be writing a letter to a specific item that meant a lot to you, expressing gratitude for its presence in your life, and then bidding it farewell. It could be simply mentally acknowledging its original importance or speaking it aloud. I remember that I had kept an assortment of childhood dolls and teddy bears. A rather big assortment! They had once been much loved and much cuddled. It was extremely hard to let go of them and each one got a kiss goodbye, a soft word, and maybe a tear in the process. This practice will help you cultivate closure and move forward with a lighter heart.

- **Space Clearing**: In addition to decluttering physical objects, consider clearing the energy in your living space. Open windows to allow fresh air and natural light to flow in. Burn cleansing herbs like sage or palo santo to purify the space. Engage in activities such as meditation, visualization, or sound healing to create an energetically balanced environment.

- **Digital Decluttering**: Extend your decluttering journey to the digital realm. Sort through your digital files, emails, and social media accounts. Unsubscribe from newsletters that no longer bring value, delete old files and photos that no longer hold significance and curate your online presence to align with your authentic self.

- **Mindful Consumption**: Shift your mindset from mindless accumulation to mindful consumption. Before purchasing new items, ask yourself if they truly align with your needs and values. Consider the environmental impact and the long-term value the item will bring to your life. Cultivate a sense of gratitude for what you already have, fostering contentment and reducing the urge to accumulate unnecessary possessions.

- **Self-Reflection Journaling**: Set aside dedicated time for self-reflection throughout your decluttering journey. Try keeping a journal to record your thoughts, emotions, and insights. Reflect on how the process is impacting your mind, body, and spirit. I also really enjoyed taking pictures along the way. I wanted to see the before and after once all the hard work was done. This brings into perspective the real distance that you travel and helps you celebrate your successes. I also used them to remind us of how far we had let our living space fall into disarray. A powerful reminder and incentive to keep it tidy. Overall the practice of keeping a record deepens your self-awareness and helps you uncover patterns and beliefs that may be contributing to the clutter in your life.

- **Movement and Mindfulness**: Incorporate movement and mindfulness practices into your decluttering routine. Engage in gentle stretching, yoga, or tai chi to connect with your body and release physical tension. Practice mindfulness meditation or deep breathing exercises to cultivate a calm and focused mindset. These practices help you stay present and centered as you navigate the decluttering process.

Remember, this holistic approach to decluttering is not a one-time event but an ongoing practice. Embrace the journey as an opportunity for growth, self-discovery, and self-care. By nurturing the mind-body connection, you create a harmonious living environment that supports your well-being and invites greater peace and balance into your life. **Try it, don't discount it!** I found that these practices actually work. By trying them out you will soon discover the ones that work best for you.

Chapter Three

Emotional Attachment and Letting Go

"The first step in crafting the life you want is to get rid of everything you don't."
- Joshua Becker[1]

Introduction to Attachment and Letting Go

Welcome to Chapter 3 of "Home Decluttering Done Best for Success!" In this chapter, we dive into the fascinating area of emotional attachment and its profound impact on our ability to declutter our homes effectively. Understanding the psychology behind our attachment to possessions is essential before embarking on the journey of decluttering. By exploring the emotional ties we have to our belongings, we can navigate the decluttering process with greater clarity and compassion.

---

1. Becker, J. (2016). The More of Less: Finding the Life You Want Under Everything You Own. WaterBrook.

It's no secret that possessions hold immense meaning for us. Over time, they become infused with memories, emotions, and a sense of identity. Each item we own tells a story, reminding us of cherished moments, relationships, or milestones in our lives. It's this emotional connection that makes decluttering such a challenging endeavor.

But why is it important to address emotional attachment before we even begin to declutter? The answer lies in recognizing that our attachment to possessions can hinder our progress. It can cause us to hold onto items we no longer need or love, resulting in cluttered spaces that drain our energy and limit our growth potential. By gaining insight into the underlying reasons for our attachment, we empower ourselves to make thoughtful decisions about what to keep and what to let go of.

The psychology of attachment is multifaceted. We may experience a fear of letting go, rooted in concerns about losing cherished memories, betraying our past selves, or feeling a sense of guilt. These emotions can manifest as anxiety, reluctance, or indecisiveness, impeding our ability to create a harmonious living environment. However, with awareness and a kind compassionate approach, we can navigate these challenges and find peace in the decluttering process.

Throughout this chapter, we will explore effective strategies for identifying sentimental items and making thoughtful decisions about them. I will guide how to differentiate between items that genuinely bring us joy and those that merely hold us captive in the past. By embracing a mindset of intentionality and self-reflection, we can release our emotional attachment to possessions that no longer serve us, freeing up space for new experiences and opportunities.

Remember, decluttering is not about erasing the past or disregarding meaningful connections. It's about creating an environment that supports and uplifts us in the present moment. So, let us embark on this transformative journey together. By understanding the emotional ties we have to our possessions, we can release their grip and discover the liberating power of letting go.

In the following sections, we will examine the psychology of emotional attachment and the sometimes overwhelming fear of letting go. I will provide practical strategies for identifying sentimental items and making thoughtful decisions about what to keep and what to finally let go of. By embracing these insights and techniques, I promise you that you will find the strength and clarity needed to declutter your home and create a space that truly reflects your authentic self.

Get ready to unlock the hidden potential of your living environment as we explore the world of emotional attachment and the valuable art of letting go.

The Impact of Emotional Attachment

Understanding our emotional attachment to possessions is a pivotal step in our journey toward decluttering our homes. Our belongings hold a significant place in our hearts and minds, as they become intertwined with our memories, experiences, and sense of self. Each item carries a story, reminding us of who we are, where we've been, and the people we hold dear. It's this emotional connection that often makes it so challenging to let go and declutter.

Recognizing the impact of emotional attachment is crucial because it influences every aspect of the decluttering process. When we are emotionally attached to our possessions, we tend to hold onto them even when they no longer serve a purpose or bring us joy. We create emotional bonds with our belongings, imbuing them with sentimental value that can make it difficult to envision our lives without them.

This attachment can manifest in various ways. We may hold onto items because of their perceived monetary value, fearing that letting go means losing something of worth. We may also cling to objects due to the memories associated with them, fearing that releasing them would erase a part of our past. And there's the fear of regret, the worry that we might discard something we'll later wish we had kept. Something that we may need in the future.

However, it's important to realize that emotional attachment can hinder our growth and well-being. Cluttered spaces drain our energy, create visual chaos, and limit our ability to focus and thrive. Our attachment to possessions can keep us tied to the past, preventing us from embracing the present and the future. By understanding the emotional hold our belongings have on us, we gain the power to make intentional choices and create a home environment that supports our current aspirations.

To embark on a successful decluttering journey, it's essential to approach our emotional attachment with understanding and gentle compassion. Rather than dismissing our feelings or rushing through the process, we must acknowledge and honor the emotions that arise as we confront our belongings. By doing so, we create space for growth, self-reflection, and positive transformation.

Understanding emotional attachment also helps us differentiate between the items that truly bring us joy and those that are simply burdening us. It allows us to assess whether our possessions align with our current values, goals, and vision for our lives. By developing a deeper awareness of the emotional ties we have to our belongings, we can make thoughtful decisions about what to keep and what to let go of, empowering ourselves to make choices that we feel positive to stand by.

In the upcoming sections of this chapter, I will guide you through strategies to identify sentimental items and provide techniques to help you make thoughtful choices during the decluttering process. Remember, it's not about erasing the past or dismissing the significance of our belongings. It's about creating a space that uplifts and supports us in the present.

So, let us embrace the journey of exploring our emotional attachment to possessions. Together, we will navigate the challenges, gain clarity, and create a living environment that nurtures our well-being and reflects the essence of who we are.

Attachment Psychology and the Fear of Letting Go

It's important to explore the underlying psychology that drives our reluctance to let our possessions go. By understanding the psychological factors at play, we can gain valuable insights into our behaviors and develop strategies to navigate the decluttering process with far greater ease.

I want to emphasize that understanding the psychology behind attachment does not diminish the significance of our emotions or imply that we should disregard our sentimental connections. Rather, it allows us to approach the decluttering journey with a compassionate and informed mindset, enabling us to make conscious choices that align with our current goals and values.

Attachment, in psychological terms, refers to the deep emotional bond we form with objects or people. It is a fundamental part of being human and serves as a means of connecting to the world around us. Our possessions become repositories of memories, emotions, and identity. They hold the power to trigger a range of emotions, from joy and nostalgia to grief and longing.

One psychological aspect that influences our attachment to possessions is the endowment effect. This cognitive bias suggests that we attribute greater value to things simply because we own them. It explains why parting with an item can be difficult, even when its practical usefulness has diminished. We may overestimate the emotional and functional value of our belongings, leading to resistance of letting go. Think of just how many times that you have said to yourself "Ahh, that might come in handy". And I bet it never has and you are still holding on to it. We had three Kettles in storage. Three! And one didn't even work.

Another psychological phenomenon tied to attachment is loss aversion—the strong preference to avoid losses over acquiring gains. We are wired to avoid the pain of losing something, even if the potential gain outweighs the loss. This loss aversion can make it challenging to part with possessions, as we fear regretting our decision or experiencing a sense of loss.

The fear of letting go is often rooted in the unknown and uncertainty about the future. Our possessions provide a sense of security and familiarity, and letting go can disrupt our comfort zone. We might worry about losing a part of ourselves, our identity, or our connection to cherished memories. However, it's really important to recognize that our true essence and memories reside within us, rather than solely in the physical objects that we possess.

Understanding these psychological factors allows us to approach the decluttering process with greater self-awareness and self-compassion. By recognizing that our attachment to possessions is influenced by cognitive biases and emotional responses, we can take intentional steps to navigate these challenges.

In the upcoming sections, I will provide guidance and practical strategies to help you navigate attachment and that terrible fear of letting go. We will explore techniques to identify the core emotional reasons behind our attachment, develop a mindset of abundance rather than scarcity, and cultivate self-compassion throughout the decluttering journey.

Remember, this process is deeply personal and unique to each of us. By understanding the psychology behind attachment, you will embark on a path of self-discovery and growth. Together, we will unravel the layers of emotional attachment and fear, empowering you to make choices that align with your present aspirations and create a home environment that supports your well-being.

So, let us unravel the complexities of attachment, and navigate the fear of letting go.

Identifying Sentimental Items and Thoughtful Decisions Making

Now that we have explored the emotional attachment and the psychology behind it, it's time to establish some practical guidance on how to identify sentimental items and make thoughtful decisions about what to keep and what to let go of. By approaching this process with intention and mindfulness, we can honor our emotions while creating a space that aligns with our present needs and aspirations.

Identifying sentimental items is a crucial step in the decluttering journey. These possessions hold a special place in our hearts, often associated with cherished memories, significant milestones, or meaningful relationships. It's important to acknowledge that sentimental items can evoke strong emotions, making it challenging to part with them. However, it's equally important to ensure that we are not holding onto things simply out of habit or fear.

To help you navigate this process, I would like to introduce an exercise called **"The Sentimental Item Reflection."** Just like before, try to find a quiet and comfortable space where you can reflect without distractions. Be sure to grab a notebook or journal to jot down your thoughts and feelings.

This exercise will take **over an hour.** Here's how it works:

- **Create an Emotional Inventory**: Begin by making a list of items that hold particular sentimental value to you. This could include family heirlooms, gifts from loved ones, personal mementos, or objects that remind you of significant events or experiences in your life. Take your time to recall and write down each item that comes to mind.

- **Reflect on the Emotional Connection**: For each item on your list, take time to reflect on the emotions it evokes in you. Ask yourself: What memories or experiences are associated with this item? How does it make me feel when I hold or see it? Does it align with my current values and aspirations? Is it connected to a person or a phase of life that is still significant to me? Allow yourself to explore deep into the emotional significance of each item.

- **Assess Practical Use and Space Constraints**: While sentimentality is an essential factor in deciding what to keep, it's also essential to consider the practical use and space constraints of each item. Ask yourself: Is this item currently serving a purpose in my life? Do I have the space to store and display it appropriately? Can it be repurposed somehow or digitized to save space while preserving its memory? Consider the practical implications alongside the emotional connection that you have to it.

- **Prioritize and Curate**: Based on your reflections and assessments, begin prioritizing and curating your sentimental items. Consider categorizing them into three groups: "Must-Keep," "Might-Keep," and "Let Go." The "Must-Keep" group includes items that hold deep emotional significance and align with your current values. The "Might-Keep" group consists of items that evoke mixed emotions or have practical constraints. The "Let Go" group comprises items that, upon reflection, no longer hold any significant emotional value or serve a purpose in your current life.

- **Revisit and Reassess**: After completing the initial curation, walk away and take a break then revisit your selections with a fresh perspective. This allows you to reassess your earlier decisions and ensure they truly align with your intentions. You may find that some items can be further categorized or that your emotional connection has evolved during the process.

Remember, this exercise is not about forcefully discarding sentimental items. It is about creating space for self-reflection, bringing awareness to the emotional significance of each item, and making thoughtful decisions that honor your values and aspirations. I found this exercise particularly useful when it came to what I first thought of as essential "Must-Keep" items. It allowed me to truly assess their worth and why I had kept them for so long. Taking the time to reflect, to relook with intention at the list was also a worthwhile exercise as many items moved down the categories as I prioritized space and focused on my aim to declutter. Later I repeated this exercise with Paul, my husband, whose sentimental grip on the accumulation of possessions was even stronger than my own. It allowed us to distinguish what items really were "Must-Keep" after all.

In the next section, we will explore strategies for releasing emotional attachment and finding peace in the decluttering process. By combining this guidance with the insights gained from the exercise, you will be equipped to navigate the challenges of letting go while creating a home environment that truly supports your well-being.

So, grab your journal and embark on the Sentimental Item Reflection exercise. It is a powerful tool for gaining clarity and setting the stage for the transformative journey of decluttering.

Releasing Emotional Attachment and Finding Peace

Now that we have identified sentimental items and made thoughtful decisions about what to keep and what to let go of, it's now time to explore strategies that will help us release emotional attachment and find peace in the decisions that we make. Letting go can be truly challenging, but with the right mindset and tools, we can navigate this journey gently with kindness and compassion. Here are some useful strategies:

- **Practice Mindfulness**: We have already found that mindfulness (Chapter 2) is a powerful practice that can help us develop a deeper understanding of our emotions and thoughts. As you engage in the decluttering process, practice being fully present in the moment. Notice the emotions that arise as you handle each item. Allow yourself to feel them without judgment or attachment. By bringing mindful awareness to your emotions, you can acknowledge them, honor their presence, and gradually let them go. Now complementing this with the
'Sentimental Item Reflection' exercise, integrate mindfulness into the process. As you revisit your curated items, take a few moments to sit quietly with each one. Notice the emotions that arise and observe any attachments or resistance that surface. By cultivating mindfulness, you can approach the decluttering process from a place of centeredness and clarity ensuring that the decisions that you come to are ones that you can stick to.

- **Create Rituals of Release**: Again we have already mentioned this way of processing your feelings. Creating helpful rituals that symbolize the act of releasing emotional attachment can be connected to items that have joined the "Let go" list. Remember that these rituals can be anywhere from lighting a candle or saying a meaningful mantra to just mentally acknowledging the item's positive emotional impact on our lives. These rituals provide closure, and a sense of gratitude, and allow you to honor the memories while embracing the freedom of letting go.

- **Repurpose or Digitize**: Some sentimental items hold immense emotional value, but their physical presence may not fit with your current space constraints or lifestyle. In such cases, consider repurposing or digitizing them. Repurposing involves finding alternative ways to use or display the item that better suits your needs and space. For example, transforming a sentimental piece of clothing into a quilt or turning old photographs into a digital photo album. This can be powerful and engaging, especially if, like me, you like to turn your hand to designing and arts and crafts. Digitizing sentimental items like letters, artwork, or keepsakes can also work and help preserve memories while reducing their physical space. By repurposing or digitizing, you can release the physical item whilst still keeping the essence of the memory intact.

- **Seek Support**: Decluttering can be an emotional journey, and it's important to remember that you don't have to go through it alone. Seek support from loved ones, friends, or even professional organizers who can offer guidance, empathy, and encouragement. Share your intentions and progress with them, allowing them to be a source of strength and accountability. Connecting with others who understand the emotional challenges of decluttering can provide powerful validation and a sense of community. It's super important that you don't feel that you are alone. You are certainly not! In helping others you also find that you are helping yourself and increasing your emotional self-worth. I have gained the most out of using my experiences to help others and in turn, I know that I have supported them in avoiding the emotional pain that comes with overwhelming clutter.

- **Embrace Minimalism**: Embracing a minimalist mindset can be liberating when it comes to releasing emotional attachment. Minimalism encourages us to focus on what truly matters, letting go of excess possessions that no longer serve us. As you declutter, remind yourself of the benefits of simplifying your life. Visualize the space and freedom you will gain by releasing emotional attachments to material possessions. Embrace the idea of curating a home environment that supports your well-being and reflects your values and in the process, it can enhance its design credentials.

Remember, releasing emotional attachment is a very personal and individual process. Be patient with yourself and trust your intuition as you navigate this journey. Taking breaks, revisiting decisions, or seeking additional support when needed is okay. Each step brings you closer to a home that nurtures your soul.

Stay committed to your decluttering journey, and together, we will transform your living space into a haven of joy and serenity.

Chapter Four

Creating a Decluttterng Plan

"The more you have, the more you are occupied. The less you have, the more free you are." - **Mother Teresa**[1]

The Planning Process

Welcome to Chapter 4 of "Home Decluttering Done Best for Success!" In this chapter, we will delve into the exciting process of creating a decluttering plan that will set the stage for your transformative journey over the next 90 days. But before we dive into the practical steps, let's take a moment to reflect on the valuable insights that we have gained so far and the significance of what lies ahead.

We have already explored the profound impact that decluttering can have on our lives. We acknowledged the emotional attachment we have to our possessions, learned how to identify sentimental items, used mindfulness, and discovered strategies to release emotional attachment

---

1. Teresa, M. (2007). Where There Is Love, There Is God: A Path to Closer Union with God and Greater Love for Others. Doubleday.

and find peace in the decluttering decision process. By immersing ourselves in these foundational concepts, we have laid solid groundwork for the transformative journey that awaits us.

To fully embrace this process, it is important to read the entire book before embarking on a room-by-room decluttering adventure tailored to your specific needs. This chapter serves as the vital preparation phase, equipping you with the necessary tools and mindset to approach the next 90 days uniquely, with confidence and clarity.

Creating a decluttering plan is more than just a logistical exercise—it is an opportunity to set personal intentions, define your vision, and cultivate a sense of purpose for your decluttering journey. It is about embracing the transformative power of organization and creating a living environment that supports your aspirations and nurtures your well-being.

As we venture forth, I encourage you to approach the process with positivity and open-mindedness. Embrace the potential that lies within each step of the plan. Celebrate the progress you make along the way, no matter how small it may seem. Remember, this is not a race; it is a personal journey of self-discovery and growth.

Throughout this chapter, I will be your guide, offering practical advice, proven strategies, and my unwavering support. Together, we will assess your current living environment, set achievable goals and timeframes, and define your vision for an organized home. This will enable us to create a personalized roadmap that will guide you through the next 90 days, ensuring that you stay motivated, focused, and inspired.

I encourage you to keep an open mind, trust the process, and remain committed to your decluttering journey. Remember, you have already taken the first crucial steps by acknowledging the importance of decluttering and understanding the emotional attachments that influence our relationship with our possessions.

So, let us continue this transformative adventure together. Prepare yourself for the practical steps that lie ahead, knowing that every decision you make, every item you release, and every space you reclaim will bring you closer to the harmonious, organized home you desire.

Before we dive into the intricacies of creating your decluttering plan, take a moment to sit and reflect on the journey you have embarked upon. Appreciate the progress you have made thus far, and let it fuel your motivation to continue moving forward. The exciting path to an organized home awaits you, and I am honored to be your guide.

Let's take the next step together and embrace the transformative power of decluttering.

Home Assessment and Prioritization

As we embark on our 90-day decluttering journey, it is essential to assess our current living environment and identify our decluttering priorities. This initial step will provide us with a clear understanding of where we stand and guide us in creating a customized plan that addresses your unique needs and aspirations.

Assessing Your Living Environment:

Take a moment to visualize your home as it is now. Take a slow intentional walk through each room, observing the spaces, surfaces, and storage areas. Notice the items that surround you, and pay particular attention to the emotions and thoughts that they evoke.

To gain a comprehensive perspective, consider the following aspects:

- **Physical Clutter**: Identify the areas in your home that are overwhelmed by clutter. These could be overflowing closets, cluttered countertops, or rooms filled with unnecessary belongings. Take a notepad and make a list of these spaces and acknowledge how they are impacting your daily life. Be thorough.

- **Emotional Impact**: Reflect on how each part of your living environment makes you feel. Do you experience a sense of calm and serenity, or is there a constant underlying stress caused by untidy disorganization? Is your bedroom a relaxing haven of calm where you can rejuvenate? Is your kitchen a place for exciting culinary creations? Or is that bathroom a place of overwhelm and disorganization that triggers stress? Recognize the emotional toll that clutter can have on your well-being and that of your family.

- **Functionality**: Assess the functionality of your space, one room at a time. Are there areas that hinder your daily routines or prevent you from utilizing your home to its full potential? Consider whether certain items or arrangements impede your ability to move freely and perform tasks efficiently. Does the clutter slow you down or stop you from doing the things you want?

Identifying Decluttering Priorities:

Now that you have assessed each room or area of your living environment, it is time to identify your decluttering priorities. This step will help you determine which areas require immediate attention and where you should focus your energy during the upcoming 90 days.

To establish your priorities, I invite you to undertake the following exercises:

Exercise 1: Room-by-Room Ranking Assessment (approx 45 mins)

Begin with your list of each room in your home. Take a moment to rank them in order of importance or urgency, based on your current needs and aspirations. Consider factors such as functionality, level of clutter, and the impact each space has on your daily life. You could also consider which areas would have the biggest emotional impact to encourage further efforts. This was one of my main considerations as I wanted to create proof points of success, mostly for myself, but also so that I could use them to engage the rest of my family.

Next, select the top three rooms that you feel would benefit you the most from decluttering. These could be the areas that cause the most stress, inhibit your productivity, or affect your overall well-being. By focusing on these priority rooms, you can experience meaningful progress and build momentum for the rest of your decluttering journey. Keep this list safe for developing your decluttering plan of action.

Exercise 2: The Vision Board Exercise (2 hours+)

This exercise led to a far greater outcome as I started to gain enthusiasm for changes to my home environment that reached beyond the immediate decluttering need. Gather some magazines, scissors, and a large poster board or a bulletin board. Set aside some quiet time for yourself and envision your ideal living environment. What words, images, and colors come to mind when you think of a clutter-free, organized home that aligns with your values and desires? What wet's your appetite for a future perfect living space? Set your creative side free. Let your emotions and imagination soar!

Leaf through the magazines, cutting out images, quotes, and ideas that resonate with your vision. Arrange them on your vision board, allowing yourself to dream and visualize the possibilities. This exercise will serve as a constant reminder of your aspirations and will guide you in making decisions aligned with your vision. It may also spark your drive and determination to attain a future that you can now visualize, illuminating new possibilities and ideas.

By completing these exercises, you will gain a deeper understanding of your living environment and establish clear decluttering priorities. Which we will incorporate into the practical steps of decluttering each room, creating your unique plan of action.

As you embark on this transformative process, keep your vision in mind and embrace the power of intention. Know that by decluttering your physical space, you are creating room for growth, clarity, and a renewed sense of well-being. Together, we will navigate this journey, step by step, and create the organized and harmonious home you deserve.

Setting Achievable Goals and Defining Your Vision

Now that you have assessed your living environment and identified your decluttering priorities, it's time to set achievable goals and define your vision further for an organized home. By establishing clear objectives and envisioning the outcome you desire, you will create a roadmap that will guide you throughout your decluttering journey.

Setting Achievable Goals:

When it comes to decluttering, setting realistic and achievable goals is crucial. It's easy to become overwhelmed by the enormity of the task, but breaking it down into manageable steps will make the process much more attainable and satisfying. Remember, progress is progress, no matter how small.

To set achievable goals, I encourage you to consider the following:

- **Specificity**: Define your goals with precision. Rather than saying, "I want to declutter my entire house," break it down into specific areas or rooms. For example, "I will declutter the kitchen pantry," or "I will sort through my wardrobe and donate my unused clothing." Whilst there may be many goals they should all be accumulated under their specific rooms.

- **Time Frame**: Assign a reasonable time frame to each goal. This will help you stay focused and motivated. Be mindful of other commitments and responsibilities, and allocate time for decluttering accordingly. For instance, "I will dedicate two hours each weekend to decluttering the living room." Remember that we are working towards a **90-day turnaround period**. That means that you can plan your time accordingly. It also recognizes that everyone's time is not the same. I know from having two excitable children that my days are not really my days and twenty-four hours in a day shrinks considerably. Add up all of your individual goals and associated timeframes. These should be assigned to their specific areas (Rooms). Consider carefully how many hours in the day you can safely assign to decluttering. Now see what total time frame your plan is generating. If the number is below 90 days then go back and assign extra days to complex tasks knowing that in most likelihood you have underestimated the time required. Be generous to yourself. If the number generated is greater than 90 days then relook at each assigned goal and hours attributed to it. Are there overlaps or duplications? Does the time element seem reasonable or over-generous? Finally, consider how many hours per day you can assign to decluttering your home. Can this increase? Target 90 as your go-to number.

- **Measurability**: Ensure to make your goals easily measurable so that you can track your progress. This could involve quantifying the number of items or the area you plan to declutter or specifying a desired outcome. For example, "I will declutter five of my bookshelves" or "I will create a minimalist workspace by removing all of the unnecessary clutter from it." I tended to target a specific area such as "completely clear the wardrobe or the cupboard" so that I felt that I had achieved a significant result in a given space.

Defining Your Vision:

Having a clear vision of your desired outcome will inspire and guide you throughout your decluttering journey. Visualize the organized home you aspire to create and let it serve as a beacon of motivation.

To define your vision, I invite you to undertake the following exercise, inspired by my own experience:

Exercise: **Visualization (approx. 15 mins)**

Find a quiet space where you can relax and focus. Close your eyes and take a few deep breaths, allowing yourself to settle into a state of calm.

Now, imagine stepping into your ideal home—the one that reflects your values promotes tranquility, and supports your daily activities. Pay attention to the details. How does it look? How does it feel? What elements contribute to its sense of order and harmony?

As you visualize your organized home, consider the benefits such a space brings to your life. How does it enhance your well-being, reduce stress, and create space for the things that truly matter? Embrace the feelings of clarity, freedom, and peace that come with an organized environment.

Take a moment to open your eyes and reflect on your visualization experience. Capture your thoughts and emotions in a journal, if you wish, or connect it to the vision board exercise. This will help you establish a deep connection with your vision and serve as a constant reminder of the transformation you seek.

Through both setting achievable goals and defining your vision, you are taking proactive steps toward creating an organized home that will meet your aspirations. In Chapter 5, we will dive into the practical decluttering process, where you will put together your customized plan, integrating the insights you have gained from these exercises.

Remember, decluttering is not just about tidying up physical spaces; it's a journey of self-discovery and intentional living.

Creating a Personalized 90-day Plan

Congratulations on reaching this stage of creating your decluttering plan! By assessing your living environment, identifying your priorities, setting achievable goals, and defining your vision, you have laid the building blocks for the transformative journey ahead. Now, let's take the final step in preparing for the next 90 days: establishing a decluttering schedule and creating a personalized roadmap.

Where to Start:

With a clear vision and specific goals in mind, it's time to determine where you will start your decluttering journey. Reflecting on the exercises that you have undertaken so far, consider the areas that hold the most significance to you. Is there a room that consistently causes stress or hampers your daily routines? Or perhaps there's an area that holds sentimental value and requires special attention. Maybe it's a specific space that will shine a beacon of light and embolden your decluttering journey. Trust your intuition and choose a starting point that resonates with you.

Remember, there is no one-size-fits-all approach here. Each person's decluttering journey is unique and personal, and it's essential to honor your individual needs and priorities. The exercises you completed earlier, such as assessing your current living environment and defining your vision, will guide you in making a fully informed decision.

Creating Your Personalized Roadmap:

Now that you have identified your starting point, it's time to create a roadmap for the next 90 days. This roadmap will serve as a guide, helping you stay focused, and motivated, and above all keep you on track. Here's how you can do it:

- **Break it Down**: Divide your decluttering journey into smaller, manageable phases. Each phase can correspond to a specific room, area, or category of items. By breaking it down, you'll prevent overwhelm and ensure steady progress.

- **Prioritize**: Based on your goals and vision, prioritize the areas or categories you wish to tackle first. Consider factors such as functionality, emotional attachment, and the impact decluttering these spaces will have on your daily life.

- **Allocate Time**: Determine a realistic timeframe for each phase. You should already have sketched out what you consider to be a realistic time allocation. Reassess your schedule and commitments, and allocate dedicated decluttering time. Remember, consistency is key here. Even small, regular decluttering sessions can yield significant results over time. Also, consider if other commitments can be rescheduled or paused for the duration that you need. Can you delegate certain tasks that eat into your day? If this is possible then great, if not then you will be successful nonetheless.

- **Track Your Progress:** We already talked about measurement and you should have identified how you will measure each area that you will tackle and how you will do it. Now use these as you keep a record of your achievements and milestones. Celebrate each step forward, no matter how small. Congratulate yourself on each milestone met and each measurement achieved. Seeing your progress on paper or in a digital tracker will motivate you to keep going. I kept a board with a grand list of areas to tackle and actions to take. After each achievement, it gave me an overwhelming sense of joy when I lined them through and with a flourish placed a large green tick by their side!

As you establish your decluttering schedule and create your personalized roadmap, remember that these preparations are vital for the upcoming Chapter. In it, we will compile the detailed process of decluttering each room, step-by-step, ensuring a comprehensive transformation of your living spaces. The insights gained from the exercises and the roadmap you create now will seamlessly integrate into your customized decluttering plan as you add greater depth to it.

Where to finish:

Finally, you may wonder where this decluttering journey ends. While the process is ongoing, completion is marked by reaching a state of equilibrium—a balance where your physical environment aligns with your vision and supports your current desired lifestyle. It's when you can effortlessly maintain an organized home that nurtures your well-being and brings you joy.

Remember, decluttering is not a race or a one-time event. It's a mindful, lifelong practice that allows you to cultivate an intentional and harmonious living space. Embrace the journey and cherish the transformations along the way.

Perhaps "The place to end" could be a physical or symbolic affirmation. I intentionally allocated a specific space to the end of the list. I told myself that once this final area was sorted, once it was clear and well organized, I would be able to scream from the rooftops that *I had won!* If that's you then designate your final battleground to overcome and raise your flag as soon as you have conquered it!

So now you have your decluttering priorities all listed down. They have been intentionally chosen using all the tools that you have been provided. You have developed a personalized roadmap to your future and you are now well-equipped to embark on the next phase of your decluttering journey. Let's together stride forth onto the practical steps needed for your home decluttering done best in 90 days.

Chapter Five

The 90-Day Home Decluttering Program

"The secret of happiness, you see, is not found in seeking more, but in developing the capacity to enjoy less." - **Socrates**[1]

Introduction to The Program

Welcome to the really exciting part where we will work together to develop your very own, unique 90-day home decluttering program that will transform your home and your life. Here is a short recap of what you should have already compiled and collected along our journey that will define your final plan:

You've already assessed your current home environment, creating a prioritized and ranked room-by-room list. This provides a solid foundation for your 90-day plan, as it will enable you to focus on areas that require immediate attention. By setting yourself achievable, time-bound, and measurable goals, you've already set the stage for success.

---

1. Socrates. (n.d.). As cited in Jones, C.H. (2023). Home Decluttering Done Best for Success! 3 Eye Publishing.

In addition to your goals, you've defined your vision—where you want to ultimately reach. This vision will serve as a powerful motivator, a 'North star' as you will, throughout the decluttering process, reminding you of the calm, organized, and inviting space you're working towards. Keep this vision close to your heart as we embark on the next 90 days together.

To get the most out of this program you need to incorporate all of the work that you have done so far into the mix to meet and hopefully exceed your aspirations. There is no getting around it, so if you have not yet completed the tasks in the first four chapters please revisit and carry them out. In the end, it will be extremely beneficial as the 90-day program will be yours and not just someone, ...well me, telling you exactly what to do and how to do it. I will be here though to guide you through the process of room-by-room decluttering, sharing the wisdom that I've gained from my own journey. By embarking on this exciting adventure together, we're setting a powerful intention to achieve inner calm by decluttering our home.

Now, let's dive into our 90-day program for lasting organization and a clutter-free existence. Each room in your home has its unique challenges and aspirations, and we'll address them one by one. We'll first break down the process into manageable tasks, using certain elements to get you to the end. We will explore both fixed and adjustment elements to make your plan your own. These will be combined with step-by-step instructions, practical tips, and techniques tailored to each room of your home to meet your specific needs. From the living spaces where you gather with loved ones to the kitchen, bathroom, bedrooms, and other areas, we'll consider factors like storage solutions, functionality, and aesthetics. All are designed to empower you to create spaces that truly reflect who you are and enhance your well-being.

So, my friends, are you ready to reclaim control over your living spaces? Let's banish the clutter, one room at a time, and create a sanctuary where you can thrive. Let's begin!

Creating Your Unique Journey

Now, let's incorporate the actions you've already taken into our customizable 90-day decluttering program. You've determined where to start, and your room-by-room list provides the roadmap for our journey. Each room will be approached systematically, following the priorities you've already spent time establishing.

As we progress through the plan, we'll leverage the insights you've gained from your previous work. Your methods to track progress will prove invaluable as we monitor your advancements and celebrate each milestone. Remember, this journey is not solely about decluttering physical spaces; it's about the transformation happening within you as well.

Throughout the 90 days, you'll have the flexibility to adapt the plan to your specific circumstances, because life happens impacting us every moment of the day. We are all only human after all. The customizable nature of this program allows you to consider factors like your available time, energy levels, and personal commitments. You may choose to tackle one room per week or dedicate concentrated efforts to specific areas during weekends. The key is to find the rhythm that works best for you, ensuring sustainable progress without feeling overwhelmed. Remember this is a 90-day program for a reason, and that reason is you and your loved ones. It's about making your home decluttering the best for success!

There is a reason why the 'planning and doing stages' are central to this book and why there are many more learnings to be had in the chapters that follow. We as human beings want to see movement forward and discover how things work together to achieve the results that we crave. It also serves as an early affirmation that you made the right choice spending your hard-won time reading these pages and performing these tasks. My advice is to create the plan and then read to the end as the advice and support found in the second half of this book will really help you going forward.

Remember also, decluttering is not a one-size-fits-all approach. Your journey is as unique as you are, and this 90-day plan is here to support and guide you, not dictate your every move. Feel free to adapt the strategies to suit your style and preferences. This program empowers you to make decisions that align with your vision, allowing you to create a home that reflects your true self.

By the end of this 90-day decluttering journey, you'll not only have transformed your physical spaces but also gained valuable insights into your relationship with possessions. The clutter that once weighed you down will be replaced with a renewed sense of lightness, freedom, and inner peace.

Let's begin the adventure!

Fixed and Adjustable Elements

Now that you have an understanding of how the 90-day decluttering plan can be customized to your unique circumstances, let's take a closer look at how this plan works. This overview will provide you with a clear roadmap, highlighting what aspects are fixed and what elements can be adjusted to fit your needs.

The Fixed Elements:

- **Timeframe**: The plan is designed to span **90 days**, offering a structured approach to ensure steady progress. This timeframe provides the framework for our decluttering journey, allowing for a balanced and achievable pace that you will work too.

- **Room-by-Room Approach**: We'll follow a systematic and organized approach by decluttering one room at a time around your home. Your prioritized and ranked room-by-room list will guide our progress and the order of things. Each room presents its own set of challenges, and by focusing on one area at a time, we can give it the attention it truly deserves.

- **Step-by-Step Instructions**: As we tackle each room, I'll provide you with detailed step-by-step instructions, tailored to the specific challenges and requirements of that space. These instructions will serve as your compass, guiding you through the decluttering process and helping you make informed decisions about what to keep, donate, or discard.

The Adjustable Elements:

- **Time Allocation**: While the program spans 90 days, you have the flexibility to adjust how much time you dedicate to decluttering each day or week. Consider your schedule, energy levels, and commitments as well as the time-bound elements of your planning so far, to find the rhythm that works best for you to meet your goals. Whether you prefer to dedicate whole weekends to decluttering or spread the tasks throughout the week or during the evenings, the choice is yours.

- **Personalized Strategies**: The strategies, techniques, and tips provided throughout the plan can be customized to suit your personal preferences and style. You are encouraged to experiment and adapt these strategies to find what works best for you. Remember, this journey is about creating a home that reflects your true self, so feel free to infuse your personality into the process.

- **Incorporating Your Past Work**: The actions you've already taken, such as assessing your home environment, setting goals, defining your vision, and establishing progress-tracking methods, will be integrated into the 90-day plan. Your past work forms a solid foundation and will inform the decisions you make as we progress through each room. Your vision will continue to guide you, and your progress-tracking methods will help you stay motivated and celebrate your achievements.

- **Checklists**: These are your trusty sidekicks. Decluttering can sometimes feel like navigating a twisting labyrinth seemingly without end, but fear not! To inspire and motivate you along the way, consider using checklists. These simple solutions allow you to note down and address every detail of your decluttering journey. These little gems will guide you through the decluttering process, ensuring that you don't miss a beat. From tackling the coffee table (*Check!*) to conquering the bookshelf (*Check!*). Each checklist will break down the steps you need to take to achieve your goals. You can develop them yourself ensuring that they accurately reflect your personal decluttering needs. Simply take the time to slowly and intentionally review your spaces, jotting down the individual actions required to get them back to the way you want them. Be thorough, breaking down whole rooms into manageable tasks i.e. clear the coffee table, or empty the sideboard. Feel the cathartic relief as you tick each task off the list once you complete them. If you would rather use some ready-made checklists that I have prepared then you can download them absolutely free at 3eyepublishing.com.

Developing Your Plan

I strongly suggest that you get yourself a large board to copy your plan down on. This will act as your constant guide and on which you will track your progress and monitor your successes. You are now going to construct an easy-to-follow yet comprehensive table of activities to reach your goal of a beautiful clutter-free home. Let's begin!

On the top left of the page mark the start date for day 1 of your program. On the top right mark the end date for day 90. Between them enter in bold the sentence **"I COMMIT 'X' HOURS EACH DAY"**. This represents your unwavering commitment. It may be that you have committed 14 hours a week however break it down to individual days. Remember consistency and regularity are key to making sustained progress. Whatever you write here, know that you need to stick to it to achieve your goals.

Now subdivide your page into 7 vertical columns. The headings from left to right are Priority, Room, Tasks, Timescale, Total time, Measure, and Progress.

Now we will work our way down creating rows as we go.

First, enter no.1 in the priority column and enter your top room priority description in column 2 next to it. In column 3 enter all the individual tasks associated with that room based on your earlier work. Next to each task write your amended time scales. Remember that you have already gone back through your rooms and tasks to ensure that the total time based on your commitments adds up to 90 days.

Once you have listed each of the tasks with their associated timescales, write in column 5, below the last line, the total time for that room based on the sum of all tasks. Refer back to your commitment at the top of your page. For instance: If you have committed 3 hours each day and your total tasks for that room add up to 9 hours then that room will take 3 days to complete. If on the other hand, you have committed 1 hour per day it will take you 9 days. You only know how much time you can genuinely commit to and what volume of tasks are required to declutter your room. The key here is to make sure what you commit to you deliver. That way 9 hours of tasks can accurately be attributed to the right number of days. And above all, you know inside yourself that you can deliver it.

Next, revert back to each task and add a concise description of the measure of success against each in column 6. You will use this as a check that you have truly completed each task.

The last column awaits you once you have completed each task and met the measure that you decided upon. Then and only then you can add a nice big gratifying tick against each task. Now you can draw a thick line beneath them all. That was everything in priority 1's row. Now add priority 2 below and its room description next to it. Add the tasks, associated timescales, total room time, and measure descriptions.

You get the idea. Now complete your table covering every room and every task in your home. Don't be daunted by the list. You have created it for a reason. By breaking down decluttering into bite-sized chunks you can focus on achieving your goal one chunk at a time. And once you have completed all the tasks in a given room you have successfully decluttered that entire space. You can see your progress. See the ticks in the far column start to build up. Set aside some specific time to celebrate each completed room with a special treat. It's important to celebrate your successes along the way. And remember you have 90 days to complete the decluttering process.

Keep your chart up to date. Savor each successful completion. Make sure that it accurately reflects your progress to date. By taking incremental steps every single day you soon start to travel down the path to a wonderful clutter-free environment that brings calm and tranquility to your life.

Now that you have your plan we will move ourselves neatly onto the room-by-room detail. Each room has a chapter dedicated to them and their unique challenges and comes with a summary detailing its average difficulty and time factors (scored out of 5) to use as a guide. Please remember that the size of someone's home can vary dramatically as well as the proportion of it that is offered up to say sleeping or cooking. The individual rooms along with the descriptions of what to look out for can be included in your plan, in the order you have set, to meet the unique needs that you have. Think of it as a simple cut-and-paste exercise that brings with it all the tips and advice for each room bolted to your individual circumstances.

Now take a deep breath, find that board or pad, gather your determination, and follow me into the detail. It's time to create the home you deserve!

Chapter Six

Living Room

"Organizing the living room is like creating a canvas for life's moments, where comfort, style, and functionality come together." - **Peter Walsh**[1]

Introduction to The Living Room

(Complexity 3, Time 3)

Ah, the living room, where relaxation and cherished memories unfold. But what happens when your sanctuary becomes overrun by clutter, robbing you of the peace and comfort you crave? Fear not, my friend, for I'm here to guide you through the step-by-step process of decluttering and organizing your living space.

Let's take a moment to envision your ideal living room. Picture yourself sinking into a deep plush sofa, surrounded by a space that feels inviting and inclusive. Do you feel at ease, sipping wine with friends or simply holding a great conversation where everyone is relaxed and simply enjoying the atmosphere? Is this how you envision your living room? Or

---

1. Walsh, P. (2012). It's All Too Much: An Easy Plan for Living a Richer Life with Less Stuff. Free Press.

do you have other priorities for the space? Are those priorities being supported today? Or are they being hindered, restricted, and notable only by their absence in your life? Let's work together to bring your living space back to life.

Decluttering Your Living Space

Begin by scanning the room and assessing each item's rightful place. Are your sofas free from clutter? Ensure that they are clear of miscellaneous items, allowing you to fully enjoy their cozy embrace. Create designated spots for essentials like the remote control, so you never find yourself rummaging through piles of pillows in search of it again.

Next, turn your attention to the chairs—those seats of connection and conversation. Are they all available to sit on, or are they buried beneath mountains of clothes, bags, or forgotten projects? Free them from the clutches of clutter, allowing their purpose to shine once more.

Consider the layout and flow of your living space. Does it feel inclusive, with a focal point that draws people together? Try rearranging the furniture in a way that encourages conversation, with comfortable seating facing each other. Ensure that the space invites relaxation and connection, allowing you and your loved ones to come together and create lasting memories.

Now, let's address the issue of magazines and papers that seem to accumulate in every corner. Create a designated storage space for these items, whether it's a stylish magazine rack or an organized drawer. By giving them a home, you'll prevent them from taking over your living space and ensure that they are easily accessible when desired. Do you have some hidden storage options like within a footstool?

Take a moment to assess the cupboards and storage spaces around your living room. Are they overwhelmed, bursting at the seams with items that no longer serve a purpose? Be discerning in your choices and let go of unnecessary clutter. Consider the paperwork or items that sit outside their designated storage spaces. Do you truly need them? If so can they be digitized or can they find their place within the cupboards, freeing up valuable surface area? Do you have an office area or somewhere where paperwork should be filed and relocated?

How about that TV bench? Do you still hold onto old DVDs or Blu-rays that you never watch now that you stream? Or their player that has become redundant? Are they taking up valued space in drawers and cupboards that could hold things that remain visible to all? Free those spaces. Remove what has no longer a purpose. Pack away all that is on show that shouldn't be. Clear the space to allow your eyes to focus on what's important and appreciate the entertainment that your living space provides.

Lastly, let's address the sacred floor space—the foundation of your living room. Is it completely free of clutter, allowing for ease of movement and a sense of openness and freedom? Remove all unnecessary items that have found their way to the floor and create a clear path for energy and flow. Which of those items do you really need and where should they be relocated? Ensure that none return to clutter the floor space.

By addressing each of these elements, you'll transform your living room into a haven of relaxation and connection. Ensure that you refer back to your checklist as a reminder of everything that you have already decided needs to be done to free your space. As you navigate this process, also keep in mind your vision of an organized and stress-free living room. Each decision you make brings you one step closer to achieving that vision.

So, my dear reader, let's dive into the world of living room organization together. Embrace the opportunity to reclaim your relaxation haven and create a space where cherished moments can unfold. With each intentional step, you'll discover the joy and serenity that come from living in a clutter-free and harmonious living room. Let's begin this journey of transformation, one sofa, one chair, and one cherished memory at a time.

Optimizing Storage and Furniture Arrangement

Hey there, my fellow decluttering enthusiast! Now that we're knee-deep in the living room makeover, let's sprinkle some charm and practicality to make this space truly shine. Get ready for some fantastic tips on how to optimize storage solutions, arrange furniture with finesse, and create an atmosphere that radiates warmth and welcome.

- **Storage Solutions**: The Hide and Seek for Clutter. Let's face it, our living rooms tend to accumulate more things than we can keep track of. But fear not, for we have some tricks up our sleeves! Invest in nifty storage solutions that hide away the clutter while still looking super stylish. Think cute baskets or trendy boxes to stash away those rogue remotes, blankets, or random toys that seem to multiply overnight. These hidden storage gems will give your space a tidy appearance, all while wowing your guests with your organizational prowess. Consider ottomans or coffee tables with built-in storage that serve to conceal the things that you may need to get to.

- **Furniture Arrangement**: To help master the art of conversation. Picture having time with your favorite people gathered in your living room, engaging in lively conversations that flow as effortlessly as the drinks you're sipping. Ah, bliss! To achieve this, let's arrange our furniture with intention. Create cozy conversation areas by positioning your chairs and sofas to face each other. And don't forget to consider the natural focal points of the room—whether it's a roaring fireplace, a TV, or a mesmerizing piece of art. By arranging your furniture thoughtfully, you'll foster a warm and inviting atmosphere where connections can flourish.

- **Creating a Welcoming Atmosphere**: A Little Softness Goes a Long Way. What's the secret ingredient to turning your living room into a haven of comfort and coziness? Soft textures! Sprinkle plush cushions, throw blankets, and oh-so-comfy area rugs throughout the space. These irresistible elements not only provide a feast for the eyes but also invite you to sink in and relax. And let's not forget the magical powers of warm and ambient lighting! Set the mood with table lamps or string lights that cast a soft glow, making your living room feel like the sanctuary you need after a long day.

- **Personal Touches**: Let Your Personality Shine. Your living room is your canvas—time to add those personal touches that make it uniquely yours! Showcase your favorite photographs in beautiful frames, displaying memories that bring a smile to your face. Infuse the space with artwork or decor pieces that reflect your personality and passions. It's these personal touches that make your living room an extension of who you are, sparking conversations and creating a space where your loved ones feel right at home.

So, my friends, armed with these tips, you're ready to transform your living room into a welcoming oasis that's equal parts functional and fabulous. And remember, while we're working our magic, don't forget the progress you've already made! Your previous steps of assessing your home, setting goals, and envisioning your ideal space have laid the groundwork for your personal 90-day decluttering program. Incorporate them into your plan, adapting them to fit the unique needs and desires of your living room.

Let's roll up our sleeves and dance to our favorite tunes as we declutter, and infuse that living room with heaps of joy and laughter. We're on the path to creating a space that feels like a warm embrace, a place where cherished memories are made and shared. Together, we'll create a living room that radiates your style, personality, and all the love you pour into it.

Chapter Seven

Dining Room

"Decluttering the dining room is not just about tidying up; it's about creating a space that welcomes meaningful conversations, laughter, and the simple pleasure of breaking bread together." **- Joshua Becker**[1]

Introduction to The Dining Room

Complexity 2, Time 3

Welcome to the heart of shared meals and memorable gatherings—the dining room! This inclusive space sets the stage for delicious feasts, engaging conversations, and cherished moments with family and friends. In this captivating chapter, we'll embark on a journey to declutter and reorganize your dining room, revitalizing it as the centerpiece of your home. Get ready to unveil the secrets to a harmonious and inviting dining space that will leave your family and guests in awe.

Imagine stepping into your ideal dining room—a place where warmth and elegance seamlessly blend to create an atmosphere that beckons

---

1. Becker, J. (2018). The Minimalist Home: A Room-by-Room Guide to a Decluttered, Refocused Life. WaterBrook.

you to sit down and savor the delights that await. As you enter, a sense of tranquility washes over you, relieving the stresses of the day. The table, adorned with tasteful decorations, awaits the arrival of culinary masterpieces and shared laughter. The chairs invite you to take a seat and immerse yourself in the joy of connection. Can you envision this harmonious scene?

Perhaps, your dining room isn't quite there yet. Maybe it's become a catch-all for miscellaneous items, buried beneath stacks of papers and forgotten clutter. Is your dining table more of a storage surface than a place for shared meals? Is it now doing double duty as an office or a play area? Are the chairs all taken, supporting piles of paperwork instead of supporting you? Do you long for a space where organization and functionality reign, allowing you to fully enjoy the pleasures of dining and entertaining or just connecting with your family at meal times?

Fear not, my champions of order and serenity, for I have the solutions you seek. Together, we will embark on a transformative journey to declutter and reclaim your dining room. Prepare to open the doors to a new chapter of elegance and efficiency.

Dining Room Declutter

Welcome, my fellow seekers of dinner-time order, to the uplifting journey of decluttering your dining room. Join me as we unveil the secrets to reclaiming your dining space and transforming it into a haven of elegance and functionality.

Now, let me share a tale from my own dining room quest to conquer the clutter. In the heart of my home stood the dining table—a magnificent piece of furniture (Remember I said it could seat an army!). It may have been magnificent but sadly it had somehow lost its way. No longer serving its intended purpose, it had become a victim of multitasking madness. It had become a landing runway for various endeavors—a makeshift office, an impromptu crafting area, a sleeping spot for our cat, and even a playground for the children's games and puzzles. Its sheer size and enormity seemed to encourage the chaos to gravitate toward it as if it whispered, "There's plenty of room for everything!"

But fortunately, this story took a positive turn as I embarked on my mission to restore harmony and functionality. I realized that it was time to resurrect this monolith's primary function as a place of gathering, feasting, and connection. With determination, I set out to uncover its hidden potential and that of the room that surrounded it.

Now, with a vision of what your ideal dining space should look like, let us embark on our transformational journey. To do that I have listed a few important strategies below that you could try:

- **The Clear-the-Surface Challenge**: Begin by selecting a specific day dedicated to reclaiming your dining table. This is 'D' day - The dining table declutter day. Set aside a couple of hours, gather some storage boxes or bins, and prepare to tackle the clutter. Start by removing all items from the table (and chairs) and placing them in the storage boxes. As you do so, ask yourself if each item truly belongs in the dining room. Sort through the contents of the boxes, making intentional decisions about what to keep, relocate, donate, or discard. Challenge yourself to find a dedicated home for each item, ensuring that the dining table remains a clutter-free zone.

- **The Functional Zone Assessment**: Take a step back and assess the functionality of your dining room. Identify different zones within the space, such as a dining area, storage area, play area, or display area. Examine each zone and consider whether the items within them align with their intended purpose. For example, are there non-dining-related items stored in the dining room? Are there items on display that no longer bring joy or serve a purpose? Reimagine the functionality of each zone and make adjustments accordingly, ensuring that items are organized and purposefully placed. Consider too the flow of the room. Does it make sense? Is it functional and will it bring joy?

- **The Dining Room Detox**: Challenge yourself to perform a thorough decluttering session in your dining room. Set aside a dedicated weekend or several evenings grouped together to embark on this transformative journey. Begin by emptying each storage cabinet, shelf, and drawer in the dining room. Assess each item as you go and ask yourself if it is truly necessary and brings value to the space. Sort items into categories (e.g., dinnerware, linens, decor) and return only the essential and cherished items to their designated places. Consider donating or discarding items that no longer serve a purpose or bring joy. Embrace the opportunity to create a streamlined and organized dining room that allows for ease and efficiency.

Once the dining table is liberated from its miscellaneous duties, cast your gaze upon the surrounding space. Take a mindful tour of your dining room and identify areas that have fallen victim to disarray. Are there cluttered shelves, neglected corners, or overcrowded cabinets? Approach these zones of chaos with resolve, sorting through the items and making intentional decisions about their place in your revitalized dining space. Let go of the unnecessary and create designated homes for the essentials. You may discover that many items should live elsewhere but be careful not to just relocate them for fear of losing them. Take a moment to consider if any items that you are moving to other places around your home need to be kept at all. Will they add anything positive to your life or simply take away space from other things that would have?

Now, let's infuse your dining room with some personal touches that reflect your unique style and aspirations. Consider decorative elements that evoke joy and create a welcoming ambiance. Whether it's a striking centerpiece, artwork that resonates with your soul, or cherished heirlooms that weave stories of the past, allow these treasures to take center stage. Maybe you have managed to repurpose something that had deep sentimental value that would now make that fantastic focal point. In our case Paul and I had collected many photos (yes actual printed photos) over our time together. These had gathered dust in the attic (we will come to that place later!). Now they were repurposed into a tasteful and colorful montage that took center stage upon a wall. Whatever you have or use or even reuse, embrace the opportunity this process provides to curate a dining room that not only enables functionality but also sparks delight and ignites conversation.

Now remember to dust yourself down, stand back, draw in a deep breath and take a moment to revel in the newfound sense of space and serenity. Admire the transformed dining table, now liberated from its multitude of roles and clutter which now beckons to you to indulge in culinary pleasures. Embrace the possibilities that lie ahead as you prepare to create lasting memories and nourish both your body and soul.

Reorganizing Your Dining Space

Welcome to the realm of reorganization, where we unlock the secrets to optimizing your dining space with ingenious storage solutions. In this section, we'll explore the art of preserving functionality while enhancing the aesthetic appeal of your dining room. Prepare to embark on a journey of practicality and style as we guide you through reorganizing what goes into your dining space.

- **Divine Dinnerware Display**: Let's start by taking a closer look at your dinnerware and glassware. Begin by decluttering your collection, bidding farewell to chipped or mismatched pieces - let's face it you will never want to use them. Embrace the beauty of simplicity and select your most cherished and versatile sets.

Now, it's time to showcase these culinary treasures in a way that adds flair to your dining space. Consider displaying a few select pieces on open shelves or in glass-front cabinets, allowing their elegance to shine through. For larger collections, explore the world of stackable organizers, adjustable dividers, and plate stands. This not only keeps your dinnerware organized but also adds a touch of sophistication to your dining room. Remember, display what you are proud of and store away what you will still need to use. The rest ...well you decide.

- **Linen Love and Storage Savvy**: Ah, the allure of exquisite linens! Whether it's tablecloths, napkins, or runners, these delicate fabrics have the power to transform any dining experience. Begin by assessing your linen collection and bid farewell to items that have seen better days or no longer resonate with your style. Once you have curated a collection that you like, it's time to find them a designated home. Consider utilizing stylish baskets, fabric bins, or even cleverly repurposed vintage suitcases to store and organize your linens. Ensure they are easily accessible while maintaining their pristine condition. Remember, folding linens neatly not only enhance storage efficiency but also adds an elegant touch to your dining room ambiance.

- **Accessories with Purpose**: It's time to enter the realm of accessories and explore how they can elevate your dining space. Begin by decluttering decorative items that no longer align with your vision or bring you positivity. Select a few key pieces that complement the style and theme of your dining room. Delicate candle holders, beautiful centerpieces, or eye-catching wall art can create focal points and ignite conversations around the table. Embrace the power of intentional placement, allowing each accessory to shine while maintaining an overall harmonious balance. Remember, less can indeed be more when it comes to creating a visually captivating and functional dining space.

On my reorganization escapades of the dining space, I discovered an ingenious way to store and showcase my cherished glassware. I repurposed a vintage bar cart, adorned it with delicate fairy lights, and transformed it into a mobile drinks station. Quirky right, but it looks fab! Not only did it free up valuable cabinet space, but it also added a touch of glamor and convenience during gatherings. It certainly became a conversation starter and a practical solution that seamlessly blended eclectic style with functionality.

As you dive into reorganizing your dining space, remember that it's not just about tidying up or finding storage solutions; it's about infusing your dining room with your unique personality and creating an environment that invites joy and connection. Embrace the opportunity to curate a dining space that reflects your style, showcases your treasured pieces, and sets the stage for unforgettable moments shared with loved ones. Go on, have fun!

Open Plan Living

Ah, the beauty of open-plan living! Let us embark on a journey to tackle the unique challenges and opportunities that arise when your dining room becomes an integral part of an open-plan living environment. Together, we'll explore strategies to harmonize your dining area with adjacent zones, creating a seamless flow between the kitchen, living room, and beyond. Say goodbye to the limitations of compartmentalization and embrace the boundless possibilities of open-concept living.

Let's first explore the purpose behind open-plan living. It's a design concept that merges different functional areas of your home, breaking down barriers and promoting a sense of interconnectedness. The purpose is to create a fluid and versatile space that allows for effortless movement, encourages social interaction, and maximizes the use of natural light. In an open-plan living environment, your dining room becomes an integral part of the larger narrative, blending harmoniously with the surrounding areas.

Now, let's delve into some strategies and exercises to help you navigate and make the most of your open-plan living-dining space:

- **Defining Zones with Purpose**: Begin by visually defining the various zones within your open-plan living environment. While there may not be actual physical walls separating each area, you can create a sense of distinction through clever furniture placement, area rugs, and strategic lighting. Consider using a large dining table or an eye-catching chandelier to anchor and highlight your dining area. This will not only provide a focal point but also establish its presence and purpose within the larger space.

- **Cohesive Color Palette**: Unify your open-plan living environment by embracing a cohesive color palette that runs seamlessly throughout. Opt for colors that complement one another, creating a harmonious visual flow. This doesn't mean you have to paint all the walls the same color, but rather select hues that work effortlessly together. Introduce pops of color through accent pieces and textiles that tie the different zones together. This cohesive palette will create a sense of unity and balance within your open-concept space.

- **Furniture Arrangement**: When it comes to arranging furniture in an open-plan living environment, it's essential to strike a balance between functionality and aesthetics. Consider the natural flow of movement and aim to create comfortable and inviting seating arrangements. Position your dining table in a way that allows for easy access from the kitchen while maintaining a connection with the living room. This encourages seamless interaction between family members and guests, whether they are preparing meals, enjoying conversation, or simply relaxing.

With all the above in mind, you need to assess where you are today. What is stopping you from utilizing the space in the best way for you? If the answer is clutter then carry out the exercises that we have already detailed. Ensure that your storage meets your needs and that all excess has been removed. Ask yourself, do the items that I have, make me feel positive, do they add anything to the space or do they simply clutter? Do I hold onto these things out of fear of letting go?

Another restrictor could be organization. Are the areas within the open-plan living space organized as they should be? Can you find what you need? Is there a place for everything and more importantly, is everything in its place? Have you explored creative methods of organizing and storing? Have you looked at furniture pieces designed with double duty in mind, or with hidden storage as part of their DNA? There are a lot of companies out there that specialize in such design techniques whether it's for 'small space living' or just clever storage ideas. Explore your options but also make the most of what you already have. Exploring, clearing, curating and cleaning are all critical steps in the process of reclaiming your living space and making it an area that you feel proud of.

As you navigate your open-plan living-dining space, remember also that the key lies in finding a balance between connectivity and individuality. Embrace the opportunities that arise from the absence of walls, allowing your dining area to seamlessly integrate with the rest of your home. By implementing the strategies and exercises we've discussed, you'll create a dynamic and harmonious open-plan living environment that reflects your style and enhances the joy of everyday living.

Chapter Eight

Kitchen

"A decluttered kitchen is a recipe for success, where you can find what you need and create culinary masterpieces with ease." - **Martha Stewart**[1]

Introduction to The Kitchen

Complexity 5, Time 4

Welcome to the heart of the home, —the kitchen! This bustling space is where we whip up culinary delights, share meals with loved ones, and sometimes, unintentionally, create chaos. But fear not! In this section, we'll dive deep into the world of kitchen decluttering and arm you with practical solutions and exercises that you need to conquer the culinary catastrophe once and for all. Get ready to turn your kitchen into a well-organized, functional, and joyful space that will inspire your inner chef.

---

1. Stewart, M. (2017). Martha Stewart's Organizing: The Manual for Bringing Order to Your Life, Home & Routines. Houghton Mifflin Harcourt.

First, let's paint a perfect picture of this area of culinary creativity where you can literally taste the magic in the air. A place that takes center stage as you pull together a meal fit for the gods to feed and entertain your guests. A place where cleanliness and hygiene are key. Where you feel the unbound freedom to experiment with ingenious ingredients and remarkable recipes to tantalize the taste buds of your friends and family.

So is your cooking space aiding you in your culinary conjurations or simply tying your hands behind your back? Are your work surfaces free to hold all those plates of perfection or do you need to juggle each for lack of a place to put them? And what of those ingredients? Are they fresh and close at hand or do they lurk with evil menace and past their finest at the back of your overburdened shelves? It's time to take control in the kitchen and I'm here to help you rediscover the fun that room once held.

Step-by-step Kitchen Decluttering and Organizing

So here we are where the magic happens! That's the magic that comes from creating a mouthwatering dish to feed the soul. But if that soul has been feeling rather undernourished of late it could be down to the over-cluttered kitchen environment that stifles such culinary creativity. To get this room back from the brink we need to refer back to your earlier assessment. Did you take your time to observe your countertops, cabinets, and drawers? Are they bursting at the seams with pots, pans, utensils, and appliances? Does it feel like a treasure hunt every time you try to find an individual ingredient or tool amidst the clutter? Well, my friend, you're not alone. Many of us have fallen victim to kitchen calamity, but together, we will work to rise above it!

Now we need to declutter like a pro. as this room can be a bit of a complex conundrum. Let's roll up our sleeves and dive into the decluttering process, one spatula at a time.

Categorization: Start by categorizing items into three simple piles: This time name them 'Must-Keep, 'Donate/sell, and 'Toss'. As you sift through every item in there, ask yourself some soul-searching questions. Do you use it? Have you ever used it? Do you really need three can openers or a collection of novelty coffee mugs? Will three mismatched plates ever see the dining table? An avocado slicer really? By letting go of unnecessary items, you'll create space for the things that truly serve you and bring you joy in the kitchen. Keep going. It's not just cutlery and cooking utensils, what about the two juice makers, the electric whisk, or a host of electronic equipment that cram onto worktops with the frightening thought that someday they will be needed? Will they? Have they been? And if that smoothie maker has been used then how often. When was the last delicious smoothie whisked around its shiny surfaces? If you can't even recall the last time then can it make way for something that you use more often like a microwave? Does it need to take up such valuable space? The countertop is after all the prime real estate of your kitchen. So go around pulling everything out and decide what stays, what gets donated, and what gets trashed. Strive to make for a lighter, more efficient cooking environment!

Efficient Organization: A place for everything *(you need)* and everything in its place. Once you've bid farewell to all the collected excess, it's time to restore order and find a home for everything in your newly decluttered kitchen. Let's now explore practical solutions to optimize your kitchen storage. Consider adjustable shelves to maximize cabinet space and keep your pots, pans, and containers easily accessible. Maximizing the volume of your inner cabinet space with similar-sized items on a shelf. No unused space inside makes for more items stored away and out of sight. Use drawer dividers to keep utensils and cutlery neatly organized. Utilize wall-mounted racks or hooks to hang frequently used tools and create additional storage space. How about a magnetic knife rack to hold those blades tight against the wall right next to where you use them? With a designated spot for each item, you'll streamline your workflow and save precious time in the kitchen.

Aesthetics and Ambience: But wait, we're not done just yet! A well-organized kitchen should not only be functional but also visually appealing and inviting. Let's infuse your kitchen with personality and charm. Select stylish containers that not only keep your ingredients fresh but also add a touch of elegance to your countertops. If you need to have your cookware out then display them proudly like beloved works of art, showcasing your culinary passion. Bring in a touch of nature with vibrant plants, adding life and freshness to your cooking sanctuary. How about a herb tray? And whilst you're at it consider if the cabinets that you do have are the right size for the space. Can they be added to or in some cases be taken away? Does the fridge/freezer, sink and cooker sit in optimum placement to each other? Are there ways to move things around without a complete overhaul or does the fact that you are looking at your kitchen from a new perspective mean that a future kitchen replacement could be planned? You don't have to go to the full extremes of a new kitchen to make the changes needed. Simple touches as described will in themselves transform your kitchen into a clearer, well-organized space that inspires creativity and ignites joy.

Are you ready to embark on this culinary adventure, my kitchen conqueror? Let's transform your kitchen from chaos to culinary bliss. Together, we'll declutter, organize, and create a space that sparks joy, ignites creativity, and elevates your cooking experience. Dive into the solutions and exercises provided, and watch as your kitchen becomes a haven of efficiency and delight. Remember to use the checklists or create your own and get ready to savor the sweet taste of kitchen success and unleash your inner culinary maestro. Let's do this!

The Pantry Organizer

Ah, the pantry—the treasure trove of ingredients, snacks, and culinary possibilities. But let's be honest, it can also be a hotbed of chaos if left unchecked. In this section, we'll delve into the art of organizing pantry items, managing those sneaky food expiration dates, and maximizing storage efficiency. Get ready to transform your pantry into a well-ordered, functional space that brings ease and joy to your cooking adventures.

Organizing Pantry Items: First things first, it's time to bring order to the pantry pandemonium. Say goodbye to jumbled shelves and mystery ingredients hiding at the back. Let's start by categorizing your pantry items into logical groups. Group similar items together, such as grains, canned goods, sauces, and spices. Utilize clear storage containers or labeled bins to keep items neatly organized and easily visible. Are your tins all facing forward neatly showing their contents descriptions making the right one easy to find? Also, take a look at your pantry shelving. Is it maximizing space usage, are there alternative solutions that you could employ? Make sure that the floor space is clear of boxes and containers so that no trip hazards exist and everything can be reached without stepping over things. Now after all that, bask in the satisfaction of effortlessly locating that spice jar or grabbing the perfect ingredient for your recipe without rummaging through a mountain of bags and boxes.

Managing Food Expiration Dates: Bid farewell to the spoiled surprises of out-of-date products. We've all been there, an expired jar of pickles at the back of the pantry, or worse, a science project slowly developing on the top shelf away from prying eyes. Let's put an end to these unpleasant surprises and prevent food wastage. Take the time to go through your pantry and check all the expiration dates. Discard anything that is past its prime or no longer safe to consume. Place near-date items at the front and either make a mental note or better still place a sticky pad on it with the use-by date. Ask yourself how many of each item you use between shopping trips. Identify items that there is an overstock of and note down to use them over the short term. Consider using a rotating storage system, placing newer items behind older ones, and ensuring that nothing gets lost in the pantry depths. Adopt a one-out, one-in approach to purchasing, ensuring that over-ordering and wastage are eliminated. By keeping a vigilant eye on expiration dates, you'll create a pantry filled with fresh, usable ingredients.

Maximizing Storage Efficiency: In a world where space is a precious commodity, it's essential to maximize storage efficiency in your pantry and make every inch count. Take a look at your shelves and consider utilizing vertical space with adjustable shelving or stackable storage solutions. Install door-mounted racks or organizers to take advantage of often-overlooked space. Use tiered shelf inserts to create additional levels and expand your storage capacity. By making every inch count, you'll create a pantry that can accommodate all your essentials while maintaining an organized and clutter-free environment.

With these techniques, you'll conquer the pantry chaos and create a well-organized culinary haven. So roll up your sleeves, my pantry perfectionist, and let's transform your pantry into a space that not only sparks joy but also empowers your kitchen creations. Make the Kitchen and pantry areas work for you. Let's do it!

Chapter Nine

Bathroom

"Simplicity in the bathroom brings a sense of calm and clarity, making the daily routines a peaceful experience." - **Francine Jay**[1]

Introduction to The Bathroom

Complexity 3, Time 2

Welcome to the sanctuary of self-care—the bathroom! This intimate space holds the key to rejuvenation and tranquility. However, if your bathroom has become a cluttered abyss of toiletries, towels, and who-knows-what, fear not! In this section, we'll embark on a transformative journey of bathroom decluttering and organization. Together, we'll create a serene oasis where you can unwind and pamper yourself with ease.

But first, let's envisage what this room of cleanliness and personal hygiene should provide. Feel the warm water cascading down upon your skin as you step effortlessly into the shower. Reaching for the soap you

---

1. Jay, F. (2019). Lightly: How to Live a Simple, Serene, and Stress-Free Life. Houghton Mifflin Harcourt.

lather and caress your skin knowing that you have plenty of time to enjoy the warm embrace of the cleansing waters as the steam rises and you breathe in the scent of your favorite toiletries. The towel is at hand, warm and fluffy, and when you do decide to step out you know that you will be met with a clear space and a calm environment. But what if the shower is full of the children's bath time toys, or the towels sit in a pile cast to the farthest corner out of reach? Does your bathroom hold the key to your morning wake-up ritual or does it interfere with your day as you desperately search for a dry towel or a toothbrush?

Step-by-Step Bathroom Decluttering and Organization

When was the last time you found the soap laying on a windowsill or a tube of toothpaste discarded on the bathroom mat? Are your bathroom cabinet doors refusing to close on the clutter that pushes against them? And where the hell has the shampoo bottle gone?

Before we can conquer the clutter, let's take a moment to look at your assessment of the bathroom battlefield. Look around. Did you identify areas that are overwhelmed with unnecessary items? Are your surfaces cluttered with products you rarely use? Do you have expired cosmetics or medications hiding in every drawer? Do the edges of your bath groan under the weight of soaps and bottles of bubble bath? By pinpointing the problem areas, you're already one step closer to restoring order and reclaiming your bathroom sanctuary. Now reflect upon your bathroom checklist before commencing. Be sure to address every area to ensure that calmness is restored. Here are some areas to pay particular attention to:

The Counter Catastrophe: Ah, the countertop. A convenient landing pad for all manner of daily essentials. But before we know it, it becomes a cluttered chaos of toothbrushes, lotions, and wayward hair accessories. Let's regain control!

One simple solution is to designate a small tray or dish to corral frequently used items like toothpaste and hand lotion. Not only does it keep things organized, but it also adds a touch of elegance to your countertop. For those pesky hair tools, consider installing a heat-resistant holder on the inside of a cabinet door to keep them within reach but out of sight.

Tangled Tales of Towels: Towels, towels everywhere! From bath towels to hand towels and everything in between, they have a way of multiplying and overwhelming our bathroom space. But fret not, my fellow towel-tamers—we have the power to conquer this clutter.

One strategy is to streamline your towel collection by keeping only what you truly need. Donate or repurpose excess towels that no longer serve their purpose in your bathroom sanctuary. To maintain order, invest in towel hooks or racks that allow for proper drying and easy access. Place them within arm's reach of the sink, shower, or bathtub. Consider assigning different-colored towels to each family member, making it a breeze to keep track of individual towels and prevent mix-ups.

Under Sink Abyss: Ah, the mysterious abyss that lurks under the sink. A place where cleaning supplies, extra toiletries, and long-forgotten items gather and create cluttered mayhem. But fear not, for we shall navigate these depths, tease out those unused hangers-on and restore order!

Start by decluttering the under-sink area, discarding expired products, and consolidating duplicates. Utilize stackable bins or baskets to keep similar items together and maximize vertical space. Label these containers for easy identification, ensuring that everything has its rightful place. Check to see if those cleaning products need to be there or if they should join their fellows in the kitchen or utility spaces. Adopt a one-out-one-in policy to your replenishment to eliminate overstock issues that cause further clutter.

Conquering the Cabinet Clutter: Cabinets are notorious hiding places for a wide array of bathroom items, from hair products to medication and beauty supplies. Let's unravel the cabinet chaos and restore harmony.

First, assess the contents of your cabinets and discard items that are past their prime or no longer serve a purpose. Invest in small storage containers or drawer organizers to keep similar items grouped together. Use clear bins or labels to identify different categories, making it a breeze to locate what you need when you need it. Stand bottles and jars facing forward, for ease of selection.

Children's bath toys: The ultimate in the incremental expansion of bathroom clutter, the children's section of your bathroom quickly expands to consume it all. Balls, boats, and bouncy floaty things all mill around looking for areas to fill. Children are little wonders, their toys are not. Consider a bath net to hold those pesky playthings away from prying hands for safety or a carry box that stores such things once they dry. This will enable you to supply everything that your child could ever want for bathtime play time and then store it all away once it's over.

By addressing these common bathroom clutter issues head-on, you're reclaiming your bathroom oasis and transforming it into a sanctuary of order and serenity. Embrace these solutions, my fellow clutter warriors, and experience the joy of tidy and harmonious bathroom space.

Now here are some further techniques to use in your pursuit of an oasis of bathroom calm:

Sorting and Streamlining: Now that we have a clear vision of what still needs to be addressed, it's time to dive into sorting and streamlining. You can do this by categorizing your bathroom items into groups such as skincare, haircare, medications, and cosmetics. As you sift through each item, ask yourself: Do I truly need this? Has it served its purpose? Let go of expired products, duplicates, and items that no longer bring you joy or serve practical use. By streamlining your collection, you'll create space for the essentials and ensure that everything in your bathroom serves a purpose.

Creating Storage Solutions: With the unnecessary items now gone, it's time to focus on creating efficient storage solutions. Bathrooms, especially small ones, can present unique challenges when it comes to storage. Maximize the available space by utilizing shelves, baskets, or over-the-door organizers. Consider vertical storage options to make the most of your walls and maximize floor space. By assigning designated spots for each category of items, you'll eliminate the visual clutter and streamline your daily routine.

Organizing with Style and Functionality: Organizing your bathroom is not just about tidiness, it's also about infusing your style and creating a functional space. Use decorative containers or jars to store cotton balls, Q-tips, or bath salts. Consider adding hooks or towel racks, for easy access to towels and bathrobes. Keep frequently used items within arm's reach, while storing less frequently used ones in accessible but more out-of-the-way spaces such as bathroom cabinets. Consider mirrored storage units that hide unsightly clutter whilst adding the illusion of space and reflected light. By combining both style and functionality, you'll elevate your bathroom to a spa-like retreat.

Maintaining Bathroom Bliss: Congratulations! You've now successfully decluttered and organized your bathroom into a serene oasis. But the journey doesn't end here. To maintain this state of bathroom bliss, adopt simple habits like regularly purging expired items, returning products to their designated spots, and staying mindful of new additions. By staying committed to a clutter-free lifestyle, you'll ensure that your bathroom remains a sanctuary of serenity and self-care.

With these step-by-step instructions, you can embrace your bathroom transformation and create a space that caters to your well-being. Your journey to bathroom serenity begins now!

Maximizing Storage, Organizing Toiletries, and Creating a Spa-Like Ambiance

Welcome back, my fellow bathroom enthusiasts! In this section, we'll explore to a deeper level some ingenious tips and tricks to maximize your storage in even the smallest of spaces, master the art of organizing toiletries, and infuse your bathroom with a spa-like ambiance. Get ready to unlock the secrets to a functional and blissful bathroom experience!

Maximizing Storage in Small Spaces: Ah, the challenge of a small bathroom—it's something many of us can relate to. But fear not, my friends, for where there's a will, there's a way! Let's harness our creativity and make the most of every inch in your compact bathroom.

One practical tip is to take advantage of vertical space. Install shelves or cabinets that extend from floor to ceiling, providing ample storage for towels, toiletries, and other essentials. Don't forget the often underutilized space above the toilet—a perfect spot for a wall-mounted cabinet or floating shelves.

One item that I found to work particularly well in our overcrowded bathroom was the over-the-door organizer. This handy storage solution swallowed toiletries, brushes, and even a hair dryer without occupying any additional space. It's a game-changer that keeps everything within reach and frees up precious countertop space. So, explore the possibilities and think outside the box—er, bathroom!

Organizing Toiletries and more with Flair: Let's face it we accumulate a myriad of toiletries over time, and without proper organization, they can quickly turn into a chaotic jumble. But fear not, for we have the power to bring order where chaos holds sway.

Consider using drawer dividers or small bins and boxes to keep similar items together, making it easy to find what you need when you need them. I've found that some open-top kitchen containers work just as well in the bathroom setting.

Does your toilet roll holder support one or six rolls and if only one, what space do the others take up?

Do all your cosmetics sit in the bathroom when you could place them in a bedroom drawer or cabinet? Where do you actually use them?

Do you hold two (or more) of everything, two toothpastes, two deodorants, and two soaps? And does everyone in your family do the same? In my household that meant eight toothpaste tubes! Store these additional items elsewhere or better still don't have them in the first place. How much notice do you need to replenish a bar of soap?

Ask yourself these questions and many more when it comes to organizing what you actually 'need' to have in your bathroom environment.

Creating a Spa-Like Ambiance: Now, let's shift our focus to transforming your bathroom into a haven of relaxation and tranquility. A mini spa getaway within the comforts of your very own home. How cool is that!

Lighting plays a crucial role in creating a soothing ambiance. Opt for soft, warm lighting options, such as dimmer switches or candles, to create a serene atmosphere. Consider placing scented candles around the bathtub or diffusing essential oils to awaken your senses and promote relaxation.

Another way to elevate the spa-like experience is to incorporate natural elements. Add plants, such as a small potted fern or a vase of fresh flowers, to infuse life and freshness into your bathroom. Hang plush, fluffy towels on hooks or towel warmers for that luxurious touch. And don't forget to indulge in a plush bath mat or rug underfoot. This is a small but impactful detail that adds comfort and style to your space.

As you implement these tips and tricks, remember that your bathroom is not just a utilitarian space—it's a sanctuary of self-care. Let your imagination run wild and infuse your style into every aspect of your bathroom oasis. Whether it's the choice of candles, the selection of plants, or the arrangement of towels, let your bathroom reflect your unique taste and enhance your well-being.

With these practical tips, you're now armed with the tools to maximize storage, organize toiletries, and create a spa-like ambiance in your bathroom. Step into your transformed space and feel the weight of the world melt away as you immerse yourself in tranquility. Embrace the art of a well-organized and rejuvenating bathroom, my fellow connoisseur of calmness. Your personal spa awaits!

Chapter Ten

Bedroom

"The bedroom should be a haven of calm, free from the weight of clutter, allowing your dreams to take flight." - **Peter Walsh**[1]

Introduction to The Bedroom

Complexity 4, Time 4

Welcome to the realm of relaxation and rejuvenation—the bedroom! This sacred space holds the key to restful nights, peaceful mornings, and a sanctuary for your dreams. In this comprehensive guide, we'll embark on a journey to declutter and organize your bedroom, transforming it into a haven of serenity and tranquility. Let's dive in and unveil the secrets to a clutter-free and harmonious sleeping space.

What would be your ideal bedroom? One where you enter and feel immediately relaxed and harmonious. Where the cool calmness of your cocooning sanctuary drives out the harried and unwelcome thoughts of a bad day at work. A place where you stretch out upon your large

---

1. Walsh, P. (2018). Let It Go: Downsizing Your Way to a Richer, Happier Life. Rodale Books.

enveloping bed and nod off to blissful sleep only to awaken refreshed and rejuvenated the next morning ready to take on the challenges of a bright new day. Does your bedroom offer you that feeling of safety and security, of calmness and serenity? Or does it present a challenge even to reach the bed without falling over piles of clothes? Are your bedside tables so cluttered that you can't even see their surfaces? How does your bedroom make you feel?

Well don't worry as I have the solutions all worked out for you. Now, my bedtime defenders of a clutter-free world, let's pull back the covers for a new bedroom makeover.

Decluttering and Organizing Your Bedroom

Let's uncover the secrets to a clutter-free and harmonious sleeping space. Remember to use the checklists and assessments that you have done. These tools will help you tackle the nightmare that is bedroom clutter.

So what is the current state of your bedroom? Cast your gaze upon your surroundings. Can you get into your bed without moving mountains of possessions? Are there piles of shoes scattered across the floor? Can you see the bedroom chair beneath the accumulation of clothes? Let's look at a few solutions to tackle these to get us started.

The Sorting Ritual: To begin our decluttering adventure, let's embrace the sorting ritual. We'll start by categorizing items into the same three simple groups: Must-Keep, Donate/sell, and Discard. As you sift through each item, ask yourself the all-important question: Does it still serve a purpose in your life? If not, it's time to bid farewell and create space for the things that truly bring you joy.

Closet Space Reimagined: Ah, the closet—a treasure trove of clothing, accessories, and hidden clutter. Let's unlock its full potential and optimize every inch of space.

Begin by decluttering your wardrobe. Take a close look at each item and ask yourself if it aligns with your current style and brings you enjoyment. Do you ever wear it? Does it even fit? I confess that when I undertook this exercise and reached inside the dreaded closet I found that I had kept dozens of items that didn't even fit me. Harking back to a time before children and a far flatter belly. How many times had I looked at a dress knowing that it was now way too small and said "One day!" but by the time that day comes, I'm sure that there will be something far more fashionable. If it doesn't fit or no longer resonates with your style, donate or sell it to someone who can appreciate it more. You will not only be giving it to a new appreciable owner and possibly gaining yourself some cash in the process, but you will also be freeing up valuable space in your closet. Win, Win, Win!

Now, let's organize what's left. Group similar items together—shirts with shirts, pants with pants, dresses with. Ok, you get it. Now also organize them in color order for easy selection. Consider implementing storage solutions such as hanging organizers, shoe racks, and drawer dividers. Maximize vertical space by utilizing cascading hangers and hooks on the back of doors. Does your closet reach your ceiling? If not and you need more storage space use storage boxes and clearly label them. Finally consider seasonal rotation and store out-of-season items in separate storage areas in vacuum-sealed bags. This helps free up space and keeps your closet organized throughout the year. By taking these simple steps, you'll create a harmonious closet that makes getting dressed a breeze.

Creating a Haven for Rest and Rejuvenation: Your bedroom should be a tranquil oasis that promotes relaxation and restful sleep. Let's craft an environment that gently lulls you into a peaceful slumber.

Start by decluttering your nightstand, keeping only the absolute essentials within reach. A lamp, a book, and perhaps a small dish for jewelry should suffice. Do you need an alarm clock? Does your nightstand have storage? Embrace the power of storage solutions, such as bedside organizers or wall-mounted shelves, to keep your nighttime essentials tidy, unseen, and yet still accessible.

Consider your bedding as well. Treat yourself to soft, cozy linens that envelop you in comfort. Invest in storage solutions for extra blankets and pillows, ensuring they're neatly tucked away when not in use. Does your bed have under-storage? Do you use it or abuse it? Take a look at what's inside and decide if it stays or goes or if it needs relocating to a more fitting place.

Peaceful Ambiance: To maintain an organized and peaceful bedroom atmosphere, we must cultivate mindful habits and employ practical strategies. Here are a few tips to guide you on this path:

- **Embrace a daily tidying routine**. Set aside a few minutes each day to put items back in their designated places to restore order.

- **Practice minimalism in your bedroom**. Keep surfaces clear of unnecessary clutter and opt for simple, soothing decor that promotes tranquility.

- **Regularly assess your belongings.** Let go of items that no longer serve a purpose or bring you joy. By doing so you are making space and creating opportunities

- **Implement storage solutions.** These storage solutions are for personal items such as jewelry, accessories, and sentimental objects. Utilize drawer dividers, trays, or decorative boxes to keep them organized and easily accessible.

By incorporating these practices into your daily life, you'll maintain a clutter-free and peaceful bedroom environment that nurtures your well-being and fosters a deep sense of calm.

As you embark on this journey to declutter and organize your bedroom, remember that it's not just about creating an aesthetically pleasing space—it's about cultivating an atmosphere that supports restful sleep, relaxation, and personal rejuvenation. Allow your bedroom to become a sanctuary where you can escape the outside world and find solace within its tranquil embrace.

With each step you take, you're bringing yourself closer to the blissful realm of a clutter-free and harmonious bedroom. So, my fellow sleep enthusiasts, let's dive in and create a space that encourages dreams, restores energy, and fills your heart with serenity. Onward to a restful haven!

Creating a Relaxing Sleep Environment

Your bedroom should be a haven of tranquility, promoting restful sleep and relaxation. Let's explore some techniques that you can use to curate a sleep-friendly environment:

- **Calming color palette**: Choose soothing colors for your bedroom walls, bedding, and decor. Soft blues, gentle greens, or serene neutrals can create a peaceful ambiance conducive to rest and restoration.

- **Lighting for relaxation**: Install adjustable lighting options, such as dimmer switches or bedside lamps with warm-toned bulbs. This allows you to create a cozy and relaxing atmosphere, ideal for winding down before sleep.

Cocooning: A bedroom that embraces you with soft linens, plush rugs, and a feeling of escapism. Consider outside intrusions such as light and noise. Do you need blackout blinds or heavy drapes to provide a sense of calm or can you get away with light and airy solutions based on your location and surroundings?

- **Soundscapes and aromatherapy**: Explore soothing sounds or white noise devices that can help mask disruptive sounds and promote tranquility. Additionally, indulge in the gentle scents of essential oils or scented candles to create a calming aroma in your bedroom.

Organizing Personal Items:

Your bedroom is also a place for personal items, accessories, and sentimental treasures that can hold a lot of emotional value. Let's explore in deeper detail techniques to keep them organized, safe, and easily accessible:

- **Jewelry storage**: Invest in jewelry organizers, such as trays, stands, or hanging organizers, to keep your accessories tangle-free and readily available. If safety is a concern consider placement in either locked drawers or cases. Otherwise, consider displaying your favorite pieces as decorative elements.

- **Sentimental treasures**: Dedicate a special space or drawer for sentimental items like letters, photographs, or keepsakes. Organize them in labeled containers or envelopes to preserve their significance while maintaining order. Digitize where appropriate.

- **Books and reading materials**: Create a designated area for your books and reading materials. Install a small bookshelf or utilize floating shelves to display your favorite titles. Consider implementing a system to organize them by genre, author, or personal preference. If space is really limited, consider e-readers as an alternative.

- **Personal care items**: Keep your personal care items, such as hair accessories, skincare products, or grooming tools and fragrances, neatly arranged and easily accessible. Utilize baskets, organizers, or drawer dividers to maintain order.

Remember, dear readers, an organized bedroom not only brings a sense of calm but also streamlines your daily routine and promotes a more mindful and restful existence. Implement these techniques, adapting them to suit your personal preferences, and witness the transformative power they hold. Embrace the journey of creating a space that reflects your unique style, fosters serenity, and encourages your personal growth.

Chapter Eleven

Attics, Basements, and Store Rooms

"Have nothing in your house that you do not know to be useful or believe to be beautiful." - **William Morris**[1]

Introduction to Attics, Basements, and Store Rooms

Complexity 5, Time 5

Welcome to the hidden realms of nostalgia, forgotten treasures, and long-lost memories—our attics, basements, and store rooms. These spaces, often tucked away from our daily lives, hold a special place in our hearts and our homes. They are the repositories of cherished possessions, mementos from bygone eras, and fragments of our personal history. In this transformative chapter, we embark on a journey to declutter and organize these storied spaces, breathing new life into the forgotten corners of our homes.

---

1. Morris, W. (1880). Hopes and Fears for Art: Five Lectures Delivered in Birmingham, London, and Nottingham, 1878-1881. Longmans, Green, and Co.

Attics, basements, and storerooms are distinct in their nature. They serve as sanctuaries for belongings that have withstood the test of time, carefully preserved for their sentimental value. Over the years, these spaces have become havens for accumulating items that no longer have an active role in our lives. The sentimental attachment can make decluttering a challenging endeavor, as each item holds a story, a memory, or a connection to our past.

Now, we stand at the threshold of cluttered and overflowing space, aware that the journey ahead will require time, patience, and a deep dive into our personal histories. It is a voyage of rediscovery, where we will sift through the layers of time and emotion, reclaiming these spaces and freeing them from the weight of accumulated possessions.

As we approach the task of decluttering and organizing our attics, basements, and storerooms, let us remember the ultimate goal. It is not simply about creating physical space or clearing out the cobwebs. It is about honoring the memories, releasing the unnecessary, and curating a space that allows us to embrace the present while cherishing the past. We shall gently navigate this path with compassion, understanding, and a commitment to preserving what truly matters.

Decluttering the Attic, Basement, or Store Room

In the grand symphony of decluttering, the attic, basement, or store room often takes center stage as the final act. These hidden spaces, shrouded in mystery and filled to the brim with forgotten possessions, may also seem like a logical starting point for our decluttering journey. After all, these areas can serve as temporary repositories for items we encounter while decluttering the rest of our homes. However, we must tread cautiously, as the very nature of these spaces can present some unique challenges.

One downside to beginning our decluttering process in the attic, basement, or store room is its invisibility to everyone but ourselves. It is not the heart of the home where we live and breathe daily, and thus it is easy to feel disheartened after investing considerable time and effort in clearing these areas. However, do not be discouraged! Remember that this undertaking is about more than just the physical act of clearing space; it is a transformative journey that touches our emotions, memories, and sense of self. Here in the dark shadowy recesses of a lifetime of stored possessions, you are likely to find great sentiment, distant recollections, and connections to items far stronger than elsewhere. Mindful contemplation and decluttering with intention will serve you well as you navigate the emotional eddies and currents that such possessions provide.

To deliver the decluttering process successfully, let us explore some practical tips and exercises that will help guide us through the labyrinth of stored belongings:

- **Start with a vision**: Before embarking on this decluttering endeavor, take a moment to envision how you want your attic, basement, or store room to serve your needs. Picture a space that is super well organized, accessible, and filled with items that truly matter to you. This vision will serve as your guiding light throughout the process.

- **Sort with intention**: Begin by sorting items into categories, such as sentimental, useful, or obsolete. Embrace the opportunity to reminisce and reflect on the memories associated with each item. Ask yourself if the item aligns with your vision for the space and if it still holds value in your life. Be mindful of the emotions that may arise during this process and allow yourself the grace to let go when necessary.

- **The rule of three**: When confronted with items that evoke indecision, consider implementing the "rule of three." Ask yourself if you have used or needed the item in the past three years if you can easily replace it if necessary, and if it truly brings joy or utility to your life. If the answer is "no" to all three questions, it may be time to bid farewell, donate or dispose of.

- **Preserve memories, not things**: Sentimental items often hold immense emotional value, but we must remember that the memories reside within us and not within the physical objects. Consider capturing the essence of sentimental items by photographing or digitizing them, or creating a memory box with a curated selection. This way, you can cherish the memories without being burdened by excessive possessions. Also, consider repurposing the items that hold sentimental value in some way. Creating a mosaic of old collections or a montage of your greatest photos as we did. Think outside the box, there may be ingenious ways to retain old memories in new functional formats that continue to give pleasure.

My storeroom decluttering journey included the discovery of a dusty box filled with childhood toys and mementos. As I sifted through the treasures of my past, I couldn't help but feel a surge of nostalgia. Each item held a story, a memory of moments long gone. However, I realized that these items had been hidden away, gathering dust for many years, unable to bring joy or serve a purpose in my present life. With a grateful heart, I chose a few cherished keepsakes and bid farewell to the rest, allowing someone else to create new memories with them.

Remember, dear readers, the power of letting go and the freedom that comes with lightening our load. As we journey through the attic, basement, or storeroom, let us embrace the opportunity to reclaim space, honor the past, and curate a collection of belongings that truly add emotional value.

Organizing Your Attic, Basement, or Store Room

Congratulations on successfully decluttering your attic, basement, or storeroom! Now comes the exciting part—organizing these spaces to make the most of their storage potential. With clear and careful organization, we can transform these areas into efficient havens where everything has its place and is easily accessible when needed. I have included several organizational strategies below:

- **Utilize Smart Storage Solutions**: Maximize every inch of available space by using practical storage solutions. Invest in sturdy shelves, plastic bins, or labeled containers to keep items neatly sorted and easily visible. Stackable boxes and modular storage systems can be particularly helpful in optimizing vertical space. Consider covered clothes racks to help store out-of-season belongings free of dust and easy to find when the time is right. The trick is to balance accessibility with smart storage.

- **Categorize and Label**: Create a logical system by categorizing similar items together. Whether it's seasonal decorations, sentimental keepsakes, or household supplies, assign clear labels to each container. This simple step will save you a lot of time and frustration when searching for specific items in the future.

- **Create Zones**: Divide your attic, basement, or store room into distinct zones based on the types of items you're storing. For example, designate separate areas for holiday decorations, sporting equipment, or archived documents. This way, you'll always know where to find what you need and maintain a sense of order. When it comes to documents consider digitizing to save space.

- **Maintain Clear Pathways**: Ensure that you have clear pathways between storage areas, allowing easy access to different sections of the space. Avoid overcrowding or blocking passageways with excessive items. A clutter-free environment not only promotes safety but also enhances the overall functionality of the area.

Beyond these great strategies are a host of tips and tricks which may also support you in your reorganizing journey. Here is a selection for you to choose from:

- **Use vertical space**: Install ceiling-mounted racks or hooks to hang bicycles, skis, or other large items, freeing up valuable floor space.

- **Store items off the floor**: Consider utilizing wall-mounted shelves or storage cabinets to keep items off the ground and protected from damage.

- **Take advantage of clear plastic storage containers**: Transparent containers allow you to quickly identify the contents without having to open each one.

- **Illuminate your belongings**: Ensure that there is enough light in these hard-to-reach places to easily identify the things that you are looking for.

As I mentioned I found that my attic space had been packed full of sentiment as well as a lot of useless tat. Remember the 3 kettles, well add to that a couple of toasters and an old vacuum cleaner. Yep, you guessed it, the cleaner didn't work either! Anyway, the point here is that these areas hold many sentimental procrastinators. What I mean is that you are more likely here than anywhere else to back away from expunging yourself from the clutter. The following exercise may help by providing you with the time to connect whilst focusing on the reason why you are doing this:

Exercise: Sentimental Sorting (2 hours+)

- Set aside dedicated time perhaps a morning or at least a couple of hours depending upon your situation and repeat if necessary. Allocate this time slot to specifically tackle the sentimental items in your attic, basement, or store room. This exercise may require emotional reflection, so it's important to create a calm and uninterrupted environment.

- Start with a small manageable pile of sentimental items and take a moment to connect with each piece. Consider the memories associated with it and the feelings it evokes inside of you. Ask yourself if it truly brings you happiness and if it aligns with your current life.

- Sort into three categories; Must Keep, Donate/Sell, and Let Go. Keep the items that hold deep sentimental value or are truly meaningful to you. Donate or sell the items that could bring joy to someone else's life. Finally, let go of any items that no longer serve a purpose or hold positive emotions for you.

- Once you've decided which items to keep, find suitable containers or storage solutions that will protect and preserve them. Take the time to organize them with intention, arranging them in a way that makes sense to you, whether it's by theme, chronology, or personal significance.

Remember, organizing is an ongoing process. Regularly assess your storage spaces, declutter as needed, and adjust your organization system to accommodate any changes in your life.

By decluttering and organizing your attic, basement, or store room, you're not only creating functional storage spaces but also uncovering the potential for rediscovering cherished memories and creating a more harmonious living environment.

Chapter Twelve

Sustainable Decluttering and Responsible Disposal

"We do not inherit the Earth from our ancestors; we borrow it from our children." - **Native American Proverb**[1]

Introduction to Sustainable Decluttering

Welcome to the path of sustainable decluttering and responsible disposal—a topic close to my heart and one that holds immense importance in our journey towards a clutter-free and environmentally conscious lifestyle. In this chapter, we will look into the crucial role we play as individuals in reducing waste, minimizing our environmental impact, and embracing a more sustainable approach to decluttering.

Our possessions carry a story, but they also leave an imprint on the planet. From the resources consumed in their production to the waste

---

1. Native American Proverb. (n.d.). As cited in Jones. C.H, Home Decluttering Done Best for Success!, 2023, 3 Eye Publishing.

generated when they are discarded, our belongings have a direct impact on the environment. But fear not, my eco-warriors of clutter-free living, for we have the power to make a positive change.

So now let's embark on this sustainable decluttering journey together, where we not only create serene and organized spaces but also contribute to a healthier planet for generations to come. Are you ready to make a difference? Let's dive in and uncover the secrets of sustainable decluttering and responsible disposal.

Reducing Waste and Minimizing Environmental Impact

Welcome to the first part of our sustainable decluttering journey, where we'll dive deep into practical guidance on how to reduce waste and minimize our environmental impact during the decluttering process. Together, we'll challenge the throwaway culture and discover actionable strategies to make a positive difference for our planet. Let's get started!

Making Conscious Decisions

Remember to take a mindful approach when considering your possessions particularly when deciding which will be retained and which are no longer required. Once we've identified the items that we no longer need or use, let's explore sustainable alternatives to simply discarding them.

Re-selling second-life products is a good way to both gain a little cash and ensure that your unwanted product goes to someone who wants it. Thereby it will continue to give pleasure to a new owner.

If selling them is not for you then how about donating to a worthy cause? Check out local donation points and their requirements. What you want to get rid of may be just what they need and could do some real good at the same time.

Another consideration is salvaging component pieces from anything you are throwing out for future use. This could be a plug from a kettle or a hinge from a cupboard door. Many items contain components that can be reused safely to support the creation or repair of other products. Screws, buttons, towels that can become cleaning cloths, handles, and shoelaces that become plant ties. You name it, those items could support your next project or needed repair and the components themselves will take up minimal space compared to the original product.

Repairing and repurposing are also fantastic ways to extend the lifespan of our belongings and minimize waste. See below for further detail on these two approaches.

Challenging the Throwaway Culture

Our next step is to challenge the prevailing culture of disposability. Before making new purchases, consider if there are sustainable alternatives available. Borrowing or renting items, joining a local sharing group, or exploring secondhand options can reduce our ecological footprint and foster a more sustainable lifestyle.

When shopping, opt for products made from sustainable materials or those with minimal packaging. By consciously supporting eco-friendly brands and products, we send a message that sustainability matters.

Repairs and Repurposing

Before tossing an item, consider if it's repairable or could be repurposed. Repairing and repurposing can be rewarding activities that save both money and resources. Let's equip ourselves with a basic repair toolkit that includes essential items like a sewing kit, glue, screws, and tools for minor repairs. Take the time to learn simple repair techniques through online tutorials or local workshops. Not only will you extend the lifespan of your belongings, but you'll also develop new skills along the way.

When it comes to repurposing, think outside the box. I have mentioned this before but it's a great way to get creative and repurpose items for different functions. That vintage suitcase can become a unique coffee table, or those old wine bottles can transform into stylish vases. The possibilities are endless!

By incorporating these actionable steps into your decluttering process, you'll reduce waste, minimize your environmental impact, and embrace a more sustainable lifestyle. Let's join hands and embark on this transformative journey toward a more mindful and eco-conscious future.

Options for Responsible Disposal

Welcome to Part 2 of our sustainable decluttering adventure, where we'll explore the exciting world of responsible disposal. Here, we'll find various options to give our unwanted items a new purpose, whether it's through recycling, donating, or upcycling. Together, we'll make a positive impact on the environment while embracing our creativity. Let's begin!

Recycling: Giving Materials a Second Life

Recycling is an excellent way to divert waste from landfills and conserve valuable resources. Start by familiarizing yourself with your local recycling guidelines. Different materials may require separate recycling streams, so it's essential to sort them accordingly. Here are a few tips:

- Rinse and clean containers before recycling them to avoid contamination.

- Flatten cardboard boxes to save space and make recycling more efficient.

- Check if there are drop-off centers or recycling programs for specific items like electronics or hazardous materials.

- Consider recycling items beyond the basics, such as old batteries, ink cartridges, or light bulbs, which often have designated recycling programs.

Remember, recycling is a collective effort. Encourage your family, friends, and community to participate and make recycling a habit.

Donating: Sharing the Love

One person's unwanted item may be another's treasure. Donating gently used items not only reduces waste but also supports charitable organizations and helps those in need. Let's look deeper into this area and consider the following when donating:

- Research local charities, shelters, or community centers that accept donations. They often have specific guidelines for acceptable items.

- Ensure that the items you donate are clean, functional, and in good condition.

- If possible, call ahead to inquire about their current needs to ensure your donation aligns with their requirements.

- Consider donating to organizations that support causes you care about, whether it's education, healthcare, or environmental initiatives.

By donating, you extend the life cycle of your possessions while making a positive impact in your community.

Responsible Disposal: Last Resort Options

While recycling, donating, and repurposing (already mentioned) should be our primary choices, there may still be some items that have reached the end of their useful life. In these cases, it's crucial to dispose of them responsibly. Here are a few suggestions:

- Research local disposal centers or waste management facilities that handle specific types of waste, such as electronics, chemicals, or large appliances.

- Check if your community has special collection events for hazardous materials, such as paint or batteries.

- Avoid improper disposal methods, such as dumping items in regular trash bins or pouring chemicals down the drain. These actions can harm the environment.

By responsibly disposing of our items, we ensure they don't pose a risk to our surroundings and contribute to a cleaner, healthier planet.

Embrace the possibilities of responsible disposal and unleash your creativity through recycling, donating, and upcycling (Repurposing). By incorporating these practices into your decluttering journey, you'll make a significant impact on the environment and inspire others to follow suit. Together, let's create a more sustainable and vibrant world for generations to come.

Embracing a Minimalist Mindset

Welcome to the transformative realm of Part 3, where we'll peak into the power of embracing a minimalist mindset. It's time to shift our perspective and uncover the profound impact that intentional choices can have on our lives and the environment. By focusing on quality over quantity, we'll create spaces that are not only visually appealing but also deeply aligned with our values and priorities. Let's embark on this minimalist journey together!

Reflecting on Your Values

Take a moment to consider what truly matters to you. What values do you personally hold dear? By understanding your core values, you'll be able to align your possessions and living space with what brings you genuine joy and fulfillment. Here are a few tips to guide you:

- **Identify your priorities**: Determine what truly matters to you and focus on nurturing those areas of your life.

- **Clarify your purpose**: Define the purpose of each room and each item within it. Ensure that they serve a meaningful function and contribute to your overall well-being.

- **Let go of societal expectations**: Don't be swayed by external pressures or trends. Embrace what resonates with you on a personal level.

Remember, minimalism is a deeply individual journey. Your version of minimalism may differ from others, and that's perfectly fine. Embrace what aligns with your values and brings you a sense of contentment.

Thoughtful Curating

With a minimalist mindset, we curate our spaces thoughtfully, focusing on intentional and purposeful choices. Consider the following tips to create a harmonious and clutter-free environment:

- **Declutter regularly**: Make decluttering a habit by periodically reassessing your possessions. Ask yourself if each item still serves a purpose or provides happiness. If not, consider letting it go.

- **Create designated spaces**: Give each item a designated home to maintain order and make finding things effortless. Avoid overcrowding and allow for space between items to foster a sense of calm and clarity.

By curating your space with intention, you create a sanctuary that nurtures your well-being and allows room for the things that truly matter.

Clutter prevention

As we embrace a minimalist mindset, it's essential to prevent future clutter from accumulating. Consider these strategies:

- **Practice mindful consumption**: Before making a purchase, pause and ask yourself if the item aligns with your values and truly adds value to your life. Avoid impulse buys, choose quality over quantity, invest in items that are well-made and durable, and seek out sustainable and ethically made products.

- **Prioritize experiences**: Shift your focus from acquiring things to creating experiences and relationships. These intangible moments often hold more value and leave lasting memories.

- **Practice gratitude**: Regularly express gratitude for the possessions you have, acknowledging their role in your life. This practice helps foster contentment and reduces the desire for excessive accumulation.

If you adopt a minimalist mindset, you're not just decluttering your physical space; you're embracing a lifestyle that values simplicity, mindfulness, and the pursuit of genuine happiness.

By curating thoughtfully, and preventing future clutter, you're on the path toward creating a harmonious and purposeful living space. Remember, minimalism is a destination. Embrace the process and allow it to guide you toward a life filled with intention, contentment, and sustainability.

Chapter Thirteen

Program Conclusion

"Out of clutter, find simplicity." - **Albert Einstein**[1]

Day 91 Reflection

Well, my courageous readers, we have concluded this exhilarating 90-day decluttering journey. Only you will know if it really has been "Home decluttering done best for success". I truly hope that it has been, or will be, as I also hope that you will read right to the end of the book before starting out. Once you have completed the process remember to take a moment to bask in the glory of your accomplishments. See how far you have come. I am positively bursting with pride for each and every one of you who make it through the 90-day process!

If you have taken my advice and taken lots of photos along the way, It's worth spending time now to review them. Remember those daunting piles of stuff that once cluttered your living spaces? The clothes that lay abandoned across the bathroom floor, The boxes of possessions that filled every recess of your attic? Well, now they should be a thing of the

---

1. Einstein, A. (n.d.). As cited in Jones. C.H, Home Decluttering Done Best for Success!, 2023, 3 Eye Publishing.

past, with only your pictures and your painful memories to show that they ever existed. You have fearlessly faced the chaos, making tough decisions, and reclaiming your home with sheer determination. Bravo, my fellow decluttering warriors!

But let's not just focus on the physical changes, no. Let's dive deep into the magic that has taken place within your hearts and minds. Can you sense the newfound clarity and lightness in your soul? Do you feel better for letting go of the unnecessary? Do you feel a weight lifted from your shoulders? I know I did when I managed to clear the last of the clutter. I know also that my family did too. The transformation was quite astonishing as if we all had been waiting in limbo for something to change but almost fearing to start that process in case it didn't work or we floundered along the way. But once you have dived in and stayed the course then you realize that you feel reinvigorated and empowered. As if anything can be achieved. And you know what....It can. It really can! You have now created a wonderful space for serenity and mindfulness to flourish.

Life is a tapestry of moments, and decluttering has gifted you more of them. More time to pursue your passions, engage with your loved ones, and savor the simple joys of existence. You've let go of the excess and made room for what truly matters.

So, my friends, as you stand in the radiant glow of your newly organized and stress-free home, hold onto this feeling tightly. Remember that you are capable of maintaining this order and embracing the mindfulness that comes with it.

Now, take a deep breath and let the sense of accomplishment sink fully in. Allow yourself to relish in the liberation from material burdens. And as you move forward, know that you have the power to create a life of continued calm and well-being.

Oh, but this is not farewell! No, no, no! This is just the beginning. There's still more to explore, more to learn and more to embrace.

In the next part of our conclusion, we'll look into the long-term benefits of an organized life and how to keep the flame of mindfulness burning bright. So stay tuned, determined declutters, and let's continue this adventure together!

The Long-Term Benefits of an Organized and Stress-Free Home

As we conclude this remarkable journey of decluttering, let us take a moment to appreciate the profound and lasting benefits that await you, and your family, in your newfound organized and stress-free home.

Gone are the days of rummaging through cluttered drawers, searching for misplaced belongings, or feeling overwhelmed by the chaos that once surrounded you. Instead, you'll find tranquility and harmony in the simplicity of your space.

An organized home brings clarity to your mind, allowing you to focus on what truly matters in life. By decluttering and streamlining your surroundings, you open up space for creativity, productivity, and meaningful connections. No longer will your energy be drained by the weight of unnecessary possessions. Instead, you will experience a newfound lightness and freedom that will invigorate your spirit.

But it doesn't end there. The benefits of an organized home extend far beyond mere tidiness. Imagine the ease with which you navigate your daily routines. No more frantic searches for misplaced keys or forgotten appointments. Your streamlined environment will support your lifestyle, making each day more efficient, less stressful, and infused with a sense of calm.

Moreover, an organized home paves the way for personal growth and self-care. As you let go of clutter and embrace a mindful approach to your surroundings, you'll gain a deeper understanding of your desires and priorities. You'll have the space and clarity to nurture your passions, cultivate healthy habits, and create a haven that reflects your truest self.

And let us not forget the impact an organized home has on those around us. A clutter-free space invites tranquility and hospitality, creating an inviting atmosphere for loved ones and guests. By sharing your decluttering journey with others, you inspire them to embark on their own transformative paths, spreading the joy of an organized life far and wide.

So, my dear friends, as we bid farewell to this 90-day decluttering adventure, let us celebrate the long-term benefits that await you—a life of simplicity, peace, and balance. Embrace the lessons learned and carry the essence of decluttering and mindfulness with you on your continued journey toward joyous calm and well-being.

Remember, it is not just about decluttering a physical space; it is about decluttering your mind, your soul, and your life. May you find everlasting joy in the treasures that truly matter, and may your organized home be a reflection of the beautiful transformation that has taken place within you.

With heartfelt wishes for your continued success and happiness, Charity

P.S. If you have found this book inspiring and more importantly its teachings and advice have made a meaningful difference then **please provide a reader's review** and let others know. Let's get the word out there to help others escape from stress and overwhelm.

Oh and look out for further books from me. They are all designed to make a real difference to our lives and well-being. Remember that the **free downloadable 90-Day Home Decluttering process template** is available from 3eyepublishing.com

Finally, I have included a bonus Chapter for you to enjoy that continues the journey because the path to a better life never stops.

Chapter Fourteen

Bonus Chapter: Nurturing a Mindful Home

"A mindful home is a sanctuary that nurtures our well-being and supports our personal growth." - **Marie Kondo**[1]

Introduction to The Mindful Home

Welcome to the BONUS chapter for those of you who want to continue the journey with your home's development. Come on in and enter the serene world of the mindful home, where each clutter-free corner radiates tranquility and nurtures your overall well-being. In this bonus chapter, we will embark on a journey to probe into the profound impact a mindful home can have on our lives. By cultivating awareness, intentionality, and presence within our living spaces, we can create an environment that supports our physical, mental, and emotional well-being.

---

1. Kondo, M. (2019). Joy at Work: Organizing Your Professional Life. Little, Brown Spark.

A mindful home is more than just aesthetically pleasing decor or minimalistic design. It is a sanctuary that encourages us to pause, breathe, and connect with the present moment. It is a haven where we can escape the external chaos and find solace in the stillness within. By embracing the concept of a mindful home, we invite harmony, balance, and a sense of purpose into our daily lives.

The impact of a mindful home extends far beyond the physical space we inhabit. It ripples into every aspect of our being, positively influencing our thoughts, emotions, and relationships. When we create an environment that nurtures mindfulness, we cultivate a deeper connection with ourselves and the world around us.

By practicing mindfulness within the home, we become more attuned to our senses, savoring the simple joys and finding beauty in the ordinary. We learn to appreciate the gentle dance of natural light, the soothing sounds of silence, and the textures that lovingly embrace us. Our surroundings become a reflection of our inner state, encouraging a sense of calmness, clarity, and contentment.

In the following sections, we will explore practical guidance on how to infuse mindfulness into your home, from daily routines to home decor and organization. We'll discover how intentional choices, conscious awareness, and thoughtful design can transform your living space into a sanctuary of mindful living. Get ready to embark on this transformative journey and unlock the power of a mindful home.

Remember, a mindful home is not merely a destination; it is a continuous practice. It invites us to be fully present, embrace imperfections, and find gratitude in the smallest of moments. Let's embark on this path together and create a mindful home that nurtures our well-being and radiates positive energy to all who enter.

Mindfulness Practices as Daily Routines

In our exploration into the mindful home, we will delve into practical guidance on incorporating mindfulness practices into daily routines within your home environment. By infusing your daily activities with mindfulness, you can create a harmonious and nurturing atmosphere that supports your well-being. Here are some great examples:

- **Morning Rituals**: Begin your day with intention and presence. Create a morning ritual that awakens your senses and sets a positive tone for the day. Take a few moments of stillness, engage in gentle stretching or meditation, and savor a mindful cup of tea or coffee. Allow yourself to be fully present and attuned to the sensations and thoughts that arise.

- **Mindful Eating**: Transform your meals into nourishing rituals. Take notice of the textures and flavours. Chew slowly and savor each bite. Engage your senses and cultivate gratitude for the nourishment that sustains your body. Minimize distractions and fully immerse yourself in the act of eating, allowing it to become a mindful and enjoyable experience.

- **Decluttering and Simplifying**: Embrace the practice of decluttering and simplifying your living space. Clearing physical clutter will have a profound impact on your mental and emotional well-being. As you declutter, bring mindfulness to the process. Notice the attachments you have to certain items and the emotions that arise. Let go of possessions that no longer serve you to create space for clarity and tranquility.

- **Mindful Cleaning**: Transform cleaning into a meditative practice. Engage in each task with mindful attention, noticing the movements, sensations, and scents involved. Embrace the opportunity to cultivate gratitude for your home and the care you put into maintaining it. Allow cleaning to become a grounding and rejuvenating practice, connecting you to the present moment.

- **Creating Sacred Spaces**: Designate a space in your home for mindfulness and self-care. Create a cozy nook where you can meditate, practice yoga, or simply be still. Fill this space with objects that hold meaning and bring you joy. Surround yourself with soothing colors, soft textures, and natural elements to evoke a sense of calmness and serenity.

- **Digital Detox**: Establish boundaries and cultivate mindfulness in your digital life. Set aside dedicated periods each day to disconnect from screens and engage in activities that nourish your mind and soul. Embrace the quietude and allow yourself to be fully present without the constant distractions of technology.

- **Nature Connection**: Bring nature into your home and cultivate a connection with the natural world. Fill your living space with plants, open your windows to let in fresh air, and incorporate natural materials in your decor. Take moments to step outside and immerse yourself in the beauty of the natural surroundings, grounding yourself in the present moment.

Remember, mindfulness is a gentle and compassionate practice of being fully present in each moment, accepting what arises without judgment. By infusing mindfulness into your daily routines and home environments, you create a sacred space for self-reflection, growth, and well-being. As renowned mindfulness teacher, Thich Nhat Hanh reminds us, *"The present moment is the only moment available to us, and it is the door to all moments."* [2] Open the door to a mindful home and let it become a sanctuary that nourishes your body, mind, and spirit.

Relaxation, Reenergizing, and Self-Care Spaces

---

2. Nhat Hanh, T. (1999). The Miracle of Mindfulness: An Introduction to the Practice of Meditation. Beacon Press.

Let us now explore the remarkable benefits of creating designated spaces within your home that are dedicated to relaxation, reenergizing, and self-care. These spaces become havens of tranquility, allowing you to nourish your well-being and cultivate a deeper connection with yourself.

- **The Restorative Power of Relaxation**: Designating a space for relaxation is essential in our fast-paced, 'Headless chicken' lives. Whether it's a cozy corner with a comfortable chair or a serene reading nook, this space can become your refuge from the outside world. Fill it with soft blankets, plush cushions, and soothing lighting to create an atmosphere of calm. Here, you can unwind, read a book, practice mindfulness, or simply enjoy moments of stillness and reflection.

- **Invigorating Spaces for Re-energizing**: In addition to relaxation, it's important to create spaces that invigorate and re-energize you. These spaces can be designated for activities such as yoga, exercise, or creative pursuits. Clear out a corner in your home, roll out a yoga mat, and adorn the space with inspiring artwork or motivational quotes. Allow this area to inspire movement, creativity, and the revitalization of your energy.

- **Self-Care Sanctuaries**: Carving out a self-care sanctuary within your home is a profound act of self-love and nurturing. This space can be a bathroom, a dedicated beauty area, or a meditation room. Fill it with elements that promote self-care, such as scented candles, luxurious bath products, soft towels, and comfortable seating. This sanctuary becomes a sacred space where you can indulge in self-care rituals, pamper yourself, and cultivate a deep sense of well-being.

- **Mindful Workspaces**: For those who work from home or engage in creative endeavors, it's crucial to create a mindful workspace. This space should be organized, clutter-free, and designed to support focus and productivity. Personalize it with meaningful objects, inspiring artwork, and plants to bring a sense of vitality and connection to your work. Incorporate ergonomic furniture and prioritize natural light to enhance your well-being while you engage in your tasks.

- **Emotional Nurturing Areas**: Lastly, consider creating spaces that support emotional nurturing and self-expression. This could be a cozy corner for journaling, a dedicated art studio, or a space to engage in therapeutic practices such as meditation or breathwork. Fill these areas with tools that encourage emotional exploration, such as journals, art supplies, or soothing music. Here, you can dive deep into your emotions, cultivate self-awareness, and engage in healing practices that promote inner growth.

Remember, the purpose of these designated spaces is to honor your well-being, provide respite from the demands of daily life, and foster a deeper connection with yourself. Allow them to evolve organically based on your needs and interests, and be open to adapting and refining them over time.

As renowned psychologist Carl Jung once said, *"Your vision will become clear only when you can look into your own heart. Who looks outside, dreams; who looks inside, awakes."*[3] By creating designated spaces for relaxation, reenergizing, and self-care, you embark on a journey of self-discovery and awaken the beauty and potential that resides within you.

Now let us explore the transformative power of bringing mindfulness to our relationships and interactions within the home. Get ready to nurture deeper connections with loved ones and infuse your home with a sense of love and compassion.

---

3. Jung, C. G. (1961). Memories, Dreams, Reflections. Vintage Books.

Infusing Mindfulness in Your Life

Now we will dive into practical tips for infusing mindfulness into various aspects of your living space, daily routines, and relationships. These suggestions will help you create a harmonious environment that nurtures mindfulness and cultivates a deeper sense of presence and connection.

- **Mindful Home Decor**: When it comes to home decor, choose items that resonate with your values and bring you joy. Opt for natural materials, such as wood or cotton, and incorporate elements from nature, like plants or stones, to create a sense of grounding. Keep your space clutter-free and organized, as a tidy environment supports a calm and focused mind. Select artwork or decor pieces that inspire serenity and reflection, reminding you to stay present in the moment.

- **Mindful Organization**: Embrace mindful organization practices to maintain a sense of order and clarity in your home. Dedicate time each day to declutter and organize different areas, whether it's your kitchen, wardrobe, or workspace. Let go of items that no longer serve you and create intentional systems to keep things tidy. Approach the process with gratitude and mindfulness, appreciating the value and purpose of each item, while also recognizing when it's time to release them.

- **Mindful Daily Activities**: Infuse mindfulness into your daily activities to transform them into opportunities for presence and self-awareness. Whether it's preparing and enjoying meals, cleaning, or engaging in hobbies, bring your full attention to the present moment. Slow down, savor each sensation, and engage your senses fully. Notice the textures, aromas, and flavors of your food, the rhythm of your breath while cleaning, or the joy of creating something with your hands. By being fully present, even in the simplest activities, you can tap into a profound sense of gratitude and fulfillment.

- **Mindful Relationships**: Extend mindfulness beyond your individual experience and bring it into your relationships within the home. Practice active listening, offering your full presence and attention to your loved ones. Engage in open and honest communication, expressing empathy and understanding. Create rituals that promote connection, such as shared meals, game nights, or quality time in nature. Cultivate an atmosphere of respect, love, and compassion, nurturing a supportive and harmonious environment for everyone to thrive.

- **Mindful Technology Use**: In our technology-driven world, it's crucial to approach our digital interactions mindfully. Set boundaries around screen time and create tech-free zones in your home to promote presence and connection. Practice digital mindfulness by engaging consciously with technology, using it as a tool for learning, creativity, and meaningful connections. Regularly unplug and engage in activities that foster relaxation, introspection, and human connection, allowing yourself to fully recharge and reconnect with yourself and others.

Keep working towards your mindful home and mindful life.

Have fun and enjoy life. x

Charity H Jones

Acknowledgements

A huge thank you to Paul, Jess, and James who have been traveling this journey with me both physically and emotionally. Thank you for your perseverance and unyielding support.

Also, a big thank you to my friends and neighbors who have contributed their thoughts and observations to the reflections captured within this book and in those books yet to come.

Love you all

Charity x

About the Author

Charity H Jones is a sunny California-based organizing guru. With her hard-working husband Paul, two hyper-active kids, and a mischievous cat named 'Kelloggs,' Charity knows the trials of juggling a bustling household. A former home designer, with a love of philosophy, yoga, and meditation, Charity has mastered the revolutionary art of storing, organizing, and decluttering to create harmonious spaces that support fulfilling family lifestyles.

Charity's magnetic blend of expertise, compassion, and understanding will leave you inspired and ready to embark on your own transformative journey. Join her and prepare for a delightful adventure as she unlocks the potential through her writings for a healthier, happier life.